Making the Small Church Effective

Making the Small Church Effective

CARL S. DUDLEY

ABINGDON
Nashville

MAKING THE SMALL CHURCH EFFECTIVE

Library of Congress Cataloging in Publication Data

DUDLEY, CARL S   1932-
   Making the small church effective.

   Includes bibliographies and index.
   1.   Small churches.   I.   Title.
   BV637.8.D83   254   78-2221

ISBN 0-687-23044-6

Scripture quotations are from the Revised Standard Version
Common Bible, copyrighted © 1973.

Chapter 3, "Growth by Adoption," contains portions of the
author's article, "Membership Growth: The Impossible
Necessity," Copyright 1977 Christian Century Foundation.
Reprinted by permission from the July 1977 issue of *The
Christian Ministry.*

MANUFACTURED BY THE PARTHENON PRESS AT
NASHVILLE, TENNESSEE, UNITED STATES OF AMERICA

In Memoriam

HATTIE LASH DOUGLAS
Her Loving Ministries Continue

Contents

Introduction 13

Chapter 1. Perspectives on the Small Church 19

Part I. Caring 29

Chapter 2. Exercise: The Choreography
of Worship 31
Chapter 2. The Caring Cell 32
The Primary Group 32
Primary Groups in Larger Churches 34
The Single Cell of People-in-Place 35
Absent and Invisible Members 37
Social Order and Social Place 38
Miniature Multicelled Churches 39
The Implications of Social Place 40
Summary of a Caring Cell 43
For Further Reading 45

Chapter 3. Exercise: Gatekeepers
and Patriarchs/Matriarchs 46
Chapter 3. Growth by Adoption 47
The Small Church Has Grown 47
The Small Church Can't Grow 48
The Small Church Can Change
into a Larger Congregation 51
New Members Without Growth Pains 54
Gatekeepers and Patriarchs/Matriarchs 56
Reservations and Possibilities 57
For Further Reading 59

Chapter 4. Exercise: The Pastor's Study
and Professional Feelings 61

Chapter 4. Pastor/People Tensions 62
   Finances 63
   Program 65
   The Self-Image of the Pastor 68
   Power in the Small Church 70
   The Lover 71
   For Further Reading 74

Part II. Conserving 75

   Chapter 5. Exercise: A Church Shield
     or Coat of Arms 77
Chapter 5. Memory and Ministry 78
   Belonging Is a Feeling 78
   Exceptions to History 80
   Biblical Memory 82
   Abuses of Memory 83
   Uses of Memory 85
   From Memory to Ministry 86
   Church Shield and Coat of Arms 88
   For Further Reading 91

   Chapter 6. Exercise: The Silent History
     of the Church 92
Chapter 6. Places of Ministry 93
   Biblical Affirmations 94
   Place in Healing 95
   Healing Ministries 97
   This Is Love—Pass It On 99
   Silent History 100
   Exorcising Places 101
   To Make a Memorial 102
   For Further Reading 103

   Chapter 7. Exercise: A Calendar
     of Annual Church Events 104
Chapter 7. Events Worth Remembering 105
   Passages of Time 106
   Personal Transitions 109

Congregational Identity 110
Expanding Ministries 113
Caring Rhythm 114
Turf Stewardship 116
A Healthy Church 119
For Further Reading 120

Part III. Coping 121

Chapter 8. Exercise: Church Groups, Goals,
and Purposes 123
Chapter 8. The Ministry of Goals and Purposes 124
Printing the Unspeakable 127
Levels of Leadership 130
Conflict over Goals 131
Goals and Purposes 134
For Further Reading 137

Chapter 9. Exercise: Church Fellowship Circles 138
Chapter 9. Turf Types of Churches 139
Heredity and Environment 140
Turf Types: Regional and Local 143
Regional: Old First and Holy Trinity 145
Regional: Ethnic Family Church 145
Regional: The High-Commitment Church 146
Local: The Stable Parish Church 147
Local: The Growing Neighborhood Church 149
Local: The Declining Neighborhood Church 150
Fellowship Circles and Membership Doors 151
For Further Reading 156

Chapter 10. Exercise: Tensions Between
Denominations and Small Churches 157
Chapter 10. Are Denominations "Viable"? 158
Mutual Distrust 159
Denominational Perspectives 161
Denominational Resources 162
The Viable Church 164

The Problems of Money 167
Tentmaking Ministries 168
Clustering Churches 170
Local Independence 174
A Summary 175
   Small-Church Perspectives 175
   Small-Church Challenges 176
   Small-Church Resources 177
For Further Reading 178

Notes 179
Index 189

Making
the
Small
Church
Effective

Introduction

The basic difference between small churches and larger congregations exists in the human relationships among those who attend. I do not mean that numbers are illusions. Small churches struggle for membership, for money, for survival. The battle is decided, not by a change of program, but by personal feelings among those who choose to join. Church membership size is not the cause of their problems. It is the result of their values, beliefs, and personal choices.

People who attend small churches give many reasons. Some have a clear theological rationale or express a personal preference. Others have a habitual response to the rhythm of the week and the cycle of the seasons. Some have denied that they have made a conscious choice: they say, "This has always been our church." Many of these same people have chosen larger associations for the other dimensions of their lives. They find employment in larger groups, shop in larger centers, send their children to consolidated schools, and travel by mass transit. Most could have chosen a larger congregation with very little additional effort. The choice to attend no church is always an option.

This book is about the people who have chosen to belong to small congregations. It grew out of workshops with pastors and members of small congregations, along with denominational leaders, from a broad range of Christian churches: Baptist, Christian (Disciples), Episcopal, Evangelical Covenant, Lutheran, Mennonite, Presbyterian, Reformed, Roman Catholic, and United Church of Christ. The book offers resources for understanding and exercises for developing the strengths of belonging in a small church.

My own motives for working with the small church grew

from unresolved tensions within me, which I found reflected in much of the literature about small churches. On one side, we affirm that "small is beautiful." On the other side, we urge membership growth for institutional "success." But if churches grow, then they cease to be small and "beautiful." My own experience reflects this confusion.

On the positive side, I attended a small neighborhood church, even though our family belonged to Old First Church in the center of the city. One summer, when I worked on a farm, I shared with the families of that valley in the experience of the crossroads church. As a student, I served in a suburban new church development. As a seminary intern, I, with my bride, set up housekeeping in the manse of a yoked parish of three churches in mountain mining communities. In each of these experiences, I found myself in the care of a large "family" called (by outsiders) a "small church." Later in the congestion of the city, I found many of these same family feelings in the urban ethnic and racial parishes. Below the level of consciousness, the affections and afflictions of these small churches have been absorbed into my being.

The other side of my experience with small churches is not as pleasant. After ordination to the gospel ministry, I was asked to serve on a committee of our denomination that had the responsibility for dispersing supplementary funds to "struggling churches." With great diligence I reviewed the mission statements that these small churches presented to the committee. I listened to the stories of their past, and their plans for the coming year. I was impressed by the sincerity of their intention to recruit new members. They were committed to being self-sufficient "within three years, four years at the most." The first year I served on this committee, I was deeply impressed. And the second. By the third year, I began to have doubts.

I had been warned. Other members of the committee had often explained the small church in very negative language. They said that small churches were "disorganized, uncommitted, and afraid of change." The most sympathetic members of the committee suggested that small churches are "trapped in their circumstances." The more cynical members confided their considered opinion that small churches are "small of vision," and "limited in leadership." Since I had spent many satisfying years in small congregations, this information was a denial of my personal experience. Their analysis challenged the validity of my experience.

This tension continued for several years. The perennial speeches from church representatives and from committee members became as predictable as if they had been written in a script. The struggling churches needed financial aid each year, "for a little while more." The members of the committee blamed the neighborhood surrounding the church and urged renewed dedication of the leaders. The meeting became an annual ritual. Neither party understood the other, and both disliked what they found themselves doing.

This book is designed to break into that cycle of ecclesiastical condescension and dependency. We do not offer programs that have been borrowed from the ways of larger congregations. We do not retell the success stories of those few high-energy churches that attract a sort of supercharged people from a wide area, but have so little in common with the struggling, small church on the corner. We are not offering sociological analysis, ecclesiastical statistics, or theological purity. We seek only to highlight the unique gifts of ministry that are the natural strength of belonging to a small congregation.

During almost two decades since my ordination, I have felt the love of two congregations while I served as their pastor. Through family and friends, I have experienced a continuing relationship with perhaps a dozen or more other congregations. I have worked with many more congregations intensely, but briefly. From these I draw the collected personal memories that inform these pages.

Fortunately, I have been able to share with a great many more congregations in the development of the Small

Church Workshop. Through the Doctor of Ministry program of McCormick Theological Seminary, I have been able to work with several hundred active pastors in a great variety of congregations. These pastors have critically tested, refined, and reported the effect of these resources in ministry with their congregations. During this past year I have shared these materials with members and pastors from more than one thousand congregations. We have participated in Small Church Workshops with pastors and people from a wide spectrum of Christian communions, from every section of the country, and from every kind of community. They have enthusiastically tested the materials, reacted, and reshaped the tools for their own use and our further edification. The results are surprising, discouraging, and ultimately very hopeful.

We were genuinely surprised at the basic similarities among all small churches. Of course, we found many differences based on denominational background and demographic situation. Ultimately, no two churches are ever identical. But in the way that people related to one another, small congregations have more in common with other small churches than they do with larger congregations in the community, or in their denominational communion.

At the same time we were discouraged in our search for programmatic answers to small-church problems. Belonging to a small church is especially attractive and uniquely satisfying to some people. Program approaches that fit in more "successful" churches often appear self-defeating among people who had chosen to belong to a small church. We cannot assume that affirming the strength of smallness must lead to church membership growth.

Beyond the disappointment of the participants at not finding "an answer" to the problems of the small church, they found the workshops ultimately reassuring. The sessions affirmed the internal strength of the small church. It is the oldest form of Christian witness, and the most numerous expression of the Christian church. It has endured, and it is a very durable form to carry the faith in the future. It may not have the visibility of massive numbers, or the clout of great capital resources. But neither should it be a drain on the ecclesiastical welfare of the denominational largess. The small church has a partnership role to play in the religious contribution to the larger society.

The workshops were biased in support of small churches. Most of the feedback came from pastors who feel called to the small church and wish they could remain—but they also have problems. In effect, this book is not a reflection of the problems, but rather it is a reflection of the way the small church is seen by pastors and lay leaders who love it. That makes a difference.

At points in the book I have used a representative term, the "Effective Small Church." By this, I do not mean that the small church was growing in membership (though a few were) or financially self-supporting (although most were). The Effective Small Church is a composite of several churches that have stabilized in their relationship to their particular environment. They seem to have a positive attitude toward themselves, and a constructive relationship with their pastor. In a time of general decline and frequent dissension, they provide a worthy model for the Christian church.

In the preparation of this book I wish to express my special thanks to several exceedingly honest and very different critics who read the manuscript in its original form, and offered extensive and insightful comments: Margaret S. Boulden; C. Eugene Bryant; Walter G. Cornett, III; Theodore H. Erickson; Lyle E. Schaller; Lincoln Richardson; and Shirley A. Wooden. Further I appreciate the general stimulation and specific suggestions that I received from my colleagues: in McCormick Theological Seminary, Professors Robert G. Boling, Thomas C. Shafer, and Robert C. Worley; and in the Lutheran School of Theology in Chicago, Professor Robert Benne. To Tim Huberty, the typist who untangled several layers of corrections to discover usable language, I am most appreciative, especially for his good humor throughout. Since I write at home, my thanks to my family, for their interest sometimes and their willingness to leave me alone the rest of the time. Thanks also to Shirley, my wife and companion, whose steady support and sparkling insight make work into fun. Finally, thanks to the people who have shown me the meaning of Christian ministry—those who have shared their ideas in many workshops across the country, and especially those loving people with whom we shared in pastoral ministry in First Presbyterian Church of Buffalo, New York, and Berea Presbyterian Church of St. Louis, Missouri.

Chapter One

Perspectives
on the Small Church

What is a small church? Most definitions are misleading, since they obscure the character and dynamics of small churches.

The term suggests that small churches are congregations with less than average membership. Strangely, that is not the way the phrase is used. In most main-line denominations, at least 60 percent of the congregations are included among the "small" churches. *Small* is something more than a numerical description.

Small is practically defined by the available resources for an anticipated ministry. Those congregations with fewer members are usually less able to generate the human, material, and financial resources to retain an ordained resident pastor and support a full program of church activities. Reduced to a single word, *money* becomes the most frequent criterion in defining the small church. In my opinion, this is not a helpful definition, but it is the most common.

The Reverend James E. Lowrey, in describing the Episcopal Church, employs such a definition: Since 125 pledging units, or at least 250 average communicants, are necessary to generate the resources for a minimum church program, the small church may be defined as those congregations with 250 or fewer members.[1] On this basis, Lowrey continues, "43 per cent of the clergy are serving 18 per cent of the people in 62 per cent of the parishes in a situation which is programed for failure."[2] In all these statistics, the Episcopal Church is typical of main-line Protestant denominations.

Lyle E. Schaller maintains that average Sunday attendance is a much more accurate index of basic church membership. He recommends that Protestant churches averaging fewer than forty-five members a Sunday should be classified as "small."[3] Congregations above that figure should take heart that they are not small comparatively. However, Schaller also notes that the "ideal size" for a congregation with one pastor would be about 175 average Sunday attendance.[4] Anything less would have to be considered less than ideal. (Schaller places the figure at 150 average Sunday attendance for a two-church parish, at 125 for a three-church parish.) The break-even number between 45 and 175 average Sunday attendance would depend upon the capacity of the congregation to raise money, and the expectations of the pastor and congregation for adequacy of program activities.

"Small church" is defined on a sliding scale. It is based on the program expectations of the membership. A Mennonite congregation of 75 would be considered large, while the same number of communicants in a Presbyterian church would rarely be able to attract a clergyperson, or keep a building open for worship and programs. Money is the bottom line for both, depending on the amount that each congregation feels is "essential" for survival and adequate for effective ministry. The attitudes of the leadership and membership have a determinative effect upon the possibilities for a particular church. "When our perception of reality falls below what really is, . . . we will tend to make modest plans. . . . The lower our self-esteem, the more likely it is that we will concentrate on 'our problems' and on institutional survival rather than on the potentialities for ministry."[5]

The majority of Protestant churches are small, and they are everywhere. Small churches are found in every kind of community—city, suburb, and rural village; they are rich and poor and exist in every kind of cultural background. The rural small church is the unmoved image of serenity in the midst of mobile America: in summer, the crossroads church under the spreading shade tree; and in winter, the heart of the Christmas season, surrounded by driven snow and issuing a warm "Season's Greetings!" Small churches are equally ubiquitous in the urban areas. Including the storefront churches with their many tongues and languages, small churches embrace more people in the congested cities than in the scattered witness of our rural areas. Even in affluent suburban neighborhoods, small churches can be found. They are the young congregations that never grew. They are the small, intentional fellowships, issue-oriented and without walls. Small churches have taken roots everywhere.

Small churches are tenacious. Some would call them tough. They do not give up when faced with impossible problems. Neither do they experience rapid shifts of membership. Over the years, some may grow and others decline. But they are peculiarly resistant to programmed intervention from outside sources. Million-dollar programs for membership recruitment leave them relatively unaffected. In membership participation, the majority of small churches have not varied 10 percent in any given decade.

At the same time, they will not die. Often financially starved, frequently without a pastor, sometimes deprived of denominational connections, the small congregation will persevere. Many members will resist the rational proposals to "save our church" through moving, merging, yoking, or teaming. The members have faith that they can hold on "somehow." In the words of one frustrated denominational leader, "The small church is the toughest, because it won't grow and it won't go away."

Not everyone is attracted to small churches. They may be ubiquitous and tenacious, but they are not universally appealing. Most church members have chosen to associate with larger congregations that provide a full-time, resident pastor, a congregation-owned building, and a variety of programs based on age and interest groups.

Although the majority of churches are small, the vast majority of members belong to larger congregations. In main-line denominations, the average size of the congregation may vary greatly (from less than one hundred to more than three hundred), but the distribution of membership remains roughly the same: 15 percent of the largest churches reach 50 percent of the membership; 50 percent of the smallest churches serve 15 percent of the members.[6] Yet the distribution of clergy serving these two groups is about equally divided: about as many pastors work with the largest 15 percent of churches (with half the denominational membership) as work with the smallest 50 percent of congregations (with less than one fifth of the denominational membership). In addition to professionally trained and ordained clergy, the larger congregations usually have several employed persons on the church staff, including musicians, educators, secretaries, and maintenance personnel. Based on their resources and organization, larger churches often pride themselves on a "full program, with something for every member of the family."

Further, larger white congregations are more frequently located in residential neighborhoods of metropolitan areas, or in growing suburban communities.[7] Their members typically are well-educated, management-oriented, and live in single-family homes. They are the consumers for the program materials and church publications. The church literature that they receive does not ignore the small church. It simply filters "smallness" through concepts and values that are acceptable (or at least understandable) to those who buy the literature. Small churches are usually portrayed as miniature versions of the larger congregations to which the purchasers belong. The uniqueness of the small church is ignored or unknown.

Recently the small church has been discovered by the press and by denominational leadership. It is ironic that the ubiquitous majority of churches (the small congregations) needed to be "rediscovered" by the minority (the larger churches). This situation can be understood in the light of mission concerns that the whole church has experienced in the past thirty years. Protestantism has been preoccupied by two compelling concerns: growth and change. With the pent-up population exploding into new subdivisions following World War II, the church responded with a commitment to expansion and a theology of church growth. With the civil-rights encounter and the war in Vietnam, the church was moved by a theology of change and a challenging social conscience. Growth and change were the dominant themes.

Against the tide of these two issues, the small church stands firm. In a climate of growth or decay, the small church offers stability. In a conflict of conscience, the small church offers the continuity of relationships. In the 1970s, church expansion slowed, the social conflict cooled, and the small church remains unmoved. In the excitement of any given moment, the small church often appears out of phase. In moments of calm, the small church is often "rediscovered." It is not apt to engage in sudden growth, nor will it likely shake the social order. But it will remain. Small churches will continue to be the quiet majority of Protestant congregations.

History is on the side of the small church. Bigness is the new kid on the block. Historically, Protestant denominations in the United States have been comparatively small. At the time of the Civil War, the size of the average Protestant church was less than one hundred members. A few large churches were in the center of the city, or at the center of the ethnic community. By the turn of the century, the average congregation still had less than one hundred fifty members.[8] Through the nineteenth century, most of the frontier clergy received at least part of their income from non-church sources. The church was primarily a neighborhood experience, locally financed.

Two organizational changes *in this century* have affected the small church. First, denominations as such have developed a regional consciousness and have organized resources from which to project area strategies and programs. The denominational organizations have hired professional staff persons as executives, developers, and coordinators. Small churches must now relate to denominational committees and staff, not to the particular congregations and pastors to whom they might have been more personally related in a previous century. Second, a few suburban congregations have grown into very large organizations. These suburban churches now rival the dominant church (Old First) in the center of the city in the number of employed staff members and sophistication of program. The model church remained a fully programmed, financially independent congregation, served by one full-time pastor, who was a generalist to the needs of "his people." But the denominational offices and the large suburban congregations emphasized a new need: the specialist, who brought particular skills to a team of professionals. The specialist clergy served larger organizations, with greater financial resources. They set new standards far above what the small congregation might provide. The lowest salary on a staff of specialists is invariably higher than the average income for a small church pastor of the same denominational judicatory.

Organizational efficiency, often equated with bigness, dominates the self-image of the church. In some denominations, the only expansion of employment opportunities has been in organizational specialities: the denominational offices, the institutional chaplaincies, and the staff positions of larger congregations. These positions are the pacesetters for professional success and the terms of clergy compensation.

In the face of these changes, the small church is tenacious, ubiquitous, and incongruous. It does not fit the organizational model for management efficiency. It does not conform to the program expectations of "something for everyone." It does not provide expanding resources for professional compensation. It is not a "success."

Unfortunately, many people experience small churches

only when the small churches have problems. Church committees and consultants with experience in larger congregations are asked about the maladies of being small. They appear in time of crisis, like medical specialists who have never known the patient. They are experts in problems such as finance and membership growth. They come from larger churches and bring programs that have worked before, in other places. It is a compassionate deed, an honest act of charity. Sometimes the medicine works. Usually the change is not lasting, and the residue is mutual frustration.

In offering this book to the reader, I run the same risks of inappropriate analysis, unsuitable recommendations, and mutual frustration. Because I have seen the pragmatism of small-church leadership and the resilience of small-church members, I doubt if these few thoughts will abuse anyone, and I trust they will prove useful to some. I have made several assumptions in the development of this material:

First, enough has been said about the limitations and weaknesses of the small church in comparison with the larger organization. I will try to describe the small church with its own integrity and beliefs. I will not knowingly avoid problem areas, but I will try to see them in context, and not in comparison with other churches.

Second, I will stick as closely as possible to the questions raised and the insights offered by pastors and people of the small congregations, and church leaders who have worked with them over the years. Clearly, I have my personal biases and blindnesses. I wish that I were more conscious of these, but at that point I must depend upon the good judgment of the reader and the guidance of the Holy Spirit.

Third, my organization of the material is based on a particular perspective that I believe is both theologically supported and sociologically evident. I believe that small churches are different from larger organizations. They have problems in many of the same areas: money, buildings, program, personnel, outreach. But people who choose small churches approach their problems differently. The small church is not an organization; it is a group.

Fourth, I have chosen to follow one particular approach to the exclusion of many alternatives. I have tried to let the implications of the theology/sociology unfold as the book progresses. This approach has the double risk of ignoring important areas for consideration, and overstating certain perspectives on the areas considered. For my oversights on the one hand and my advocacy on the other, I warn the reader to beware. At the same time, I have consciously chosen a consistent approach in hopes that those who see and understand the problems in particular situations will take the germ of an idea or insight and let it grow very differently from anything that I had conceived or anticipated.

Specifically, the book is divided into three parts: Part 1, *Caring,* will focus on the implications of smallness in the intimacy of membership. We shall consider the implications of "primary relationships" among members who know one another perhaps too well, and have done so for perhaps too long. In such a primary group, we shall consider the prospects for membership growth, church program, and pastoral care. Part 2, *Conserving,* will explore the interaction in faith and theology among the members of small churches, and between the church and its community. We shall look at the way small churches develop character based on their perspectives of culture, time, and place. Part 3, *Coping,* will seek to distinguish the way particular congregations express their character and deal with their problems. We shall take special note of conflict in small churches, different types of congregations and the styles they express, and the interaction between small churches and denominational programs.

Since this material was generated by a series of workshops, each chapter will be introduced by an "exercise." These exercises should provide a different level of appreciation for the dynamics of small congregations. Since personal relationships lie at the heart of the small-church experience, the exercises are designed to offer to the reader a sense of personal participation and immediate application. The combination of printed text and personal exercises should point out a much more important reality, that is, to the experience of belonging in a small congregation.

Part One: Caring

To understand the small church, we begin with the feelings of the members. When asked, members show a strong sense of ownership and deep feelings of belonging. "This is *our* church," they say. Members do not begin with apologies or comparisons, unless they are implied because the questioner comes from a larger congregation. For members, the small church is not "small but beautiful," or "small but quality," or "small but anything." Members have a strong, positive attitude toward belonging, because it is a significant experience in their lives. Some "members" are not active in programs, or even regular in attendance on Sunday. They may participate only on special occasions and attend only for annual events. Some such members are not even listed on the rolls of the church, but it remains "*our* church" to them. They have remained with the church despite other alluring alternatives. In times of crises for the congregation, they have rallied with support. In the crises of their personal families, the congregation has surrounded them with care and concern. Belonging to the church is like being a member of the family.

Part 1 presents the unique character of small church *caring*. The discussion is based on the concept of the "primary relationships" that provide the strength of belonging in small churches. In chapter 2 we consider the "place" of persons in the group. The problems of growth are raised in chapter 3. Questions of program and leadership are considered in chapter 4.

Chapter Two

Exercise: The Choreography of Worship

The place of worship has accumulated meaning for those who attend. The way people enter, sit, participate, and depart is a folk dance in slow motion, a choreography of worship. In this exercise, we observe the dance of our own worship.

The exercise is best done if people work separately at first and then share preliminary results. Over a period of weeks they can test their findings by checking the seating of people throughout the sanctuary, and by talking with particular people about the meaning of their "place."

Procedure: Draw a diagram of the sanctuary, especially noting the location of the pews, the pulpit, the choir, and other seating arrangements.

Mark where you sit. (In your mind, sit there and imagine looking around.) Mark initials to indicate where other people usually sit. Add as many people as possible before you continue the exercise. Finally, put a circle around the initials of those to whom you usually speak before or after worship.

When you have gone as far as you can alone, share your diagram with others who are working on the project. You might also wish to consult a membership list of the congregation. Make a note of the people whom you remembered first, and those whom you could not remember until reminded.

With the faces, the concerns, and the prayers of these people in mind, we are ready to consider the caring qualities of the small congregation.

Chapter Two

The Caring Cell

If membership is so satisfying in small churches, then why do they not attract more people? But since it appeals to relatively few people, who have to carry such heavy burdens, they why do they give so much of themselves to keep the church open? It doesn't make sense—perhaps. The size of the small congregation can be best understood through the sociological insights of the "primary group."

The Primary Group

In a primary group, members are united by common interests, beliefs, tasks, and territory. They are not self-conscious about their relationships and are bound together more by sentimental ties than by contractual agreements. They have a solidarity, a feeling of belonging, nourished by experiences of intimacy and personal need. The primary group is a folk society in the midst of the urban culture. When so many other contacts are temporary and impersonal, the primary group provides the atmosphere of an extended family. In the often quoted words of Charles Cooley, "[Primary groups] are primary in several senses, but chiefly in that they are fundamental in forming the social nature and ideals of the individual."[1]

Like the primary group, the small church develops and confirms the ideals of individuals in the context of its own character and strength. Like the primary family group, the small church offers intimacy and reassurance among those who can be trusted. Like the extended family, many small churches have a territorial identity with a particular place. Its turf may be the rural crossroads or the urban *barrio* or the old neighborhood or even the developing suburb. Like the family-clan, the church family often carries the food, rhythm, and culture of a particular ethnic, racial, or national group.[2] The faith is transmitted through the cultural artifacts. In this caring group, people who claim a common heritage can share the rhythm of the seasons, and the silence of life's transitions.

Personal relationships are the basis of the primary group. At best, such relationships are warm, intimate, spontaneous, and personally satisfying. But not always. Primary relationships may become hot, cruel, petty, and irrational. Cooley continues, "It is not to be supposed that the unity of the primary group is one of mere harmony and love. It is always a differentiated and usually a competitive unity."[3] Primary groups have a capacity to embrace a variety of motives and enhance a wide range of "characters." People are cared for, even in the tensions of strained relationships. Primary groups may be demanding at critical moments, and may inhibit or even smother the creativity of individual members. If their relationships were contractual, members might be free to leave. But they stay, because their roots are far deeper than reason or contract. Members are held by common experiences, community caring and, according to Theodore Erickson, their "own integrity, shaped by biblical, historical and cultural roots."[4]

Primary groups typically react to their environment with a "live and let live" attitude. On the one hand, they present a solid front. Although they fight within the family, they will close ranks if approached by an outsider. Oppression increases the commitment of members to one another. Sometimes they cling to imagined oppression as a means of maintaining group solidarity.[5] At the same time, they have no need to control the environment in order to prove their identity. Members receive their satisfactions from the time shared, from being together and caring for one another. Additional achievements are almost accidental, not essential to the group.[6] Like the flower in the wall, the beauty of the group together "is its own excuse for being."

Primary Groups in Larger Churches

The small group is, of course, the building block of every congregation. Larger churches may have many such small groups to provide for mutual sharing and support. Church groups are organized around prayer, study, and service; around age groups, men's and women's interests; around the concerns of couples, families, single persons, the young, and the elderly; around planning for events, sharing social interests, enjoying recreation, engaging in social causes. In a congregation of five hundred members, half of an "average membership" will claim to belong to one or more church groups. A person who belongs to one group will usually participate in several. Many of these provide the members with the satisfactions of primary relationships in the context of the larger congregation.

Most of the denominational program materials are designed to be used in small groups and sub-groups. Usually the materials will have suggestions for ways to organize the church around various interests, tasks, skills, and objectives to accomplish the stated goals of the material. This pattern is characteristic of women's organization manuals, Christian education materials, fund-raising, membership recruitment, and even development and evaluation of worship. Task groups can become primary groups through the experience of working and sharing together.

Small group processes have been especially effective in assimilating members in churches located in communities of high mobility. Although the population may experience a rapid turnover, the churches have used small groups to develop common tasks and provide a sense of accomplishment in a common product. This can be done in a relatively short cycle, with different start-up times for the groups, resulting in waves of groups that flow through the life of the church. Small groups have become the living cells of a much larger church body.

But small churches are unique. They are not multicelled

organizations with a common base. Small churches are a single, caring cell embracing the whole congregation.

The Single Cell of People-in-Place

The small congregation is the appropriate size for only one purpose: the members can know one another personally. Not all the members can know all the others on a continuing, face-to-face basis, but they can all know about one another. They expect to be able to "place" everyone physically and socially in the fabric of the congregation. The caring cell church may be defined as a primary group in which the members expect to know, or know about, all other members.

In a specific physical sense, members can associate the name with the face, the face with the family, and the family with the place where each person sits in worship. Those people whom they do not know personally, or who may not be regular in attendance at worship, can be placed through various connections in the congregation and in the community, such as relatives, friends of relatives, neighbors and neighbor's neighbors, place of employment, home residence (maybe by the name of a former owner), length of time in the community, and so on. Everyone has a place and can be located in the fabric of the congregation.

When I have used the Choreography of Worship exercise, I have found that most people are uncomfortable when they are asked to say why they sit where they do. Those who answer quickly usually have a functional reason: "I can see better" or "I can hear better"; "So I can be available for ushering" or "To take up the collection"; "It's my seat in the choir," or "I can avoid the draft." All these sound reasonable, until we ask people to move. Then we discover there is a relationship between the person and the pew that is far more than functional.

"She was livid," said the astonished pastor, "and she is not like that. I thought she would hit him with her cane." The pastor was describing an elderly woman who found her pew preempted by a visitor. The woman later apologized and said that she did not know "what possessed me." Our reasons for our choice of pew may sound rational to us, but after a time we become attached to "our place." If people are frustrated in reaching their place, they become quite anxious; if asked to move, they become downright hostile. "The territorial principle motivates all of the human species," says Robert Ardrey,[7] and we remember the gentle woman with her cane in the air.

Most people cannot say exactly why they sit where they do, or why they would not feel right if they worshiped in another pew. But they usually can remember the names of the people who have shared that pew with them, and who first brought them to that spot. One father said that he used to sit across the church, and his son sat in this pew. But his son went to Vietnam and never returned, so "I like to sit where he did before he left home." One young man said, "This is where we have always sat," but he is new to the congregation and his family is a thousand miles away. In a congregation with a long history, one older woman said that she was unwilling to move because "I might be sitting in someone's pew, although of course they have mostly died. Still, it is their place. . . ." One gentleman said he sat where he did simply "because it is my seat."

A minority of people do not take one consistent location. Some will sit in one of two or three choices. If pressed, they will usually recall the faces of those with whom they have shared those places, and moving is almost like visiting. Others seem to want to "float" to visit with people, and to provide for their own need for "personal space."[8] Even without a place, their space has a sense of others, a relationship to the worshiping community.

The pew and the sanctuary as a whole can be seen as people-space. Through the mixture of faces and experiences, empty space and physical objects begin to take on a sustained significance in our lives.[9] The act of worship becomes a "folk dance" in slow motion, a graceful gliding of people seeing the familiar and touching the friendly as they enter, take their places, renew their sense of the Lord's loving care, and "depart in peace." As one sensitive pastor said of an old, stiff congregation, "Everyone is in the procession, not just the choir!" It is the choreography of worship, as regular and as beautiful as any dance on stage.

When do the members arrive, and what is their pattern of entry? What reason do they offer for their seating, with whom do they visit, and what is their pathway of departure? The choreography of worship may say more about a member's theology than all the scripture learned and creeds recited. Further, the dance with its fixed positions and locations of the people may say more of the history and commitments of the congregation than all the printed chronicles.

Absent and Invisible Members

Physical place has a special impact on the sense of well-being among the members of the congregation. The presence of people in their places creates a positive climate for congregational activities. The absence of someone is felt by many others in the congregation. When someone is not in his or her place, others *feel* the absence. Thus the pastor of an urban ethnic congregation notes, "Those who attend worship know everyone else, to whom they are related, and where they work; and they become very anxious when someone misses a worship service." The empty pew in worship has much the same impact as the empty chair at the evening meal of a large family: everything may be all right, but the family feels incomplete.

The member who missed worship is apt to be called, not just to be reminded that someone cares. He or she is reprimanded for being absent, because the absence "hurt" the pattern of seating in worship. Others *felt* the absence and respond, sometimes in anger.

At the same time, there are other people in worship who may be "invisible." The Choreography of Worship can be a very disturbing exercise to the pastor, and to the elders, deacons and vestry when we discover that some people are "invisible"—that is, they are not even remembered as part of the worship experience. This is the typical response of using the exercise in a larger congregation: fewer people have fixed seats, and most people only remember their stratum (age-friendship) of the congregation. But in the caring cell of the small church, the officers should be able to place all the regular worshipers. The ones forgotten are often those who most need the care of the congregation: the elderly who sit alone, the young people who seek some independence, and the children who are quietly part of the family (the noisy children and youth are remembered first, with negative feelings). Priority of memory offers insight into the caring style of the congregation.

Seating in the sanctuary is symbolic of the caring cell. Everyone has a place in the fabric of the group. The group is whole (*shalom,* at peace) when the people are present.

Social Order and Social Place

The experience of belonging to a small congregation meets a basic human need for social order and metaphysical orderliness. Order, says Peter Berger, is "a protective structure of meaning, erected in the face of chaos. Within this order the life of the group as well as the life of the individual makes sense. Deprived of such order, both the group and individual are threatened with the most fundamental terror, the terror of chaos that Emil Durkheim called *anomie* (literally, a state of being 'order-less')."[10] In the small congregation, the rhythm of the week begins and ends with every thing and every person to be found in his or her rightful place. Berger continues:

Man's propensity for order is grounded in a faith or trust that, ultimately, reality is "in order," "all right," "as it should be." Needless to say, there is no empirical method by which this faith can be tested. To assert it is itself an act of faith. But it is possible to proceed from the faith that is rooted in experience to the act of faith that transcends the empirical sphere. . . . In this fundamental sense, every ordering gesture is a signal of transcendence.[11]

Ordering of events and people can be seen as the backbone, the hard skeleton, for the life of the social body. The pulse of routine events and the placing of particular people provides the framework within which life is predictable and people are cared for. "At the very center of the process of becoming fully human, at the core of *humanitas,* we find an experience of trust in the order of reality," Berger affirms.[12] Ordering and caring are two sides of the same coin. Once order has been affirmed, Christian caring can embrace a larger community.

Members of small churches "place" people in more than their seats in the sanctuary. The small church is often only the formal gathering of a much larger community, sometimes only the tip of the iceberg. Members have a social place, not just in the church but also in the larger community: they are known by family—to whom they are related, to whom they were related, and sometimes to whom they ought to be related. A few members in a relaxed evening can draw relationships (sociometrics) between almost everyone on the parish list, and often even more people who are not on the list. The small church retains the "village sensitivity" to people, even in the most urban setting. Perhaps especially in the city, the church provides the ties to the social turf. Members care for those who have made confession and communion, and for many more. They care for the families of families and "to all that are far off" (Acts 2:39). They care for the whole "village."

Miniature Multicelled Churches

Not all churches with fewer than two hundred members are single cells of caring Christians whose members expect to know one another personally.[13] For example, Old First Church or Old Holy Trinity may have been caught in the backwash of changing communities. Typically, Old First

Church will have a few members, a large building, and many empty rooms. Often it will continue to print a full roster of church groups, with something for everyone and a leader for every group. But the population has changed, the membership shrunk, and the groups no longer meet. It may be a small church in size of membership, but it remains a multicelled organization. It limps along with unfilled cells. The key difference is in the attitude of the members. They do not expect to know everyone and do not feel the need to place everyone who comes in the door. They have many cells, but without enough members. They cherish their memories.

The multicelled church is typically open and waiting. The single-cell church is less open but more durable. The multicelled church is designed for diversity and expansion. The single-cell church is more appropriate for caring, and surviving. In the hostile environment of a culturally changing community, the multicelled church must be sustained from outside sources, or it will die.

In this chapter we shall introduce four implications of the simple, caring cell that will be expanded in subsequent chapters. First, the caring cell provides an arena for healing and for caring. Second, the intensity of concern forces some delineation of boundaries between people; these may appear as social distance or even hostility. Third, the caring cell provides its own cocoon for time and space. Fourth, social space is difficult to enter. Because these themes are interdependent, we shall introduce them together and then consider them separately.

The Implications of Social Place

(1) Beneath the sense of wholeness when people are "in place" lies a concern for the physical health as well as the presence of members. When the absence of a person "hurts," then health is not an idle concern. How are you? is a question, not just a social greeting. The one who asks must have time for an answer. For the busy pastor or

committee chairperson, no business can be transacted until the question of health has been settled.

Caring has a healing effect upon the one cared for and upon those who initiate the caring. Caring has a way of putting our lives in perspective, our priorities in place. Milton Mayerhoff, in his little book *On Caring,* describes the effect:

In the context of a man's life, caring has a way of ordering his other values and activities around it. When this ordering is comprehensive, because of the inclusiveness of his carings, there is a basic stability in his life; he is "in place" in the world. . . . My feeling of being in-place is not entirely subjective and it is not merely a feeling, for it expresses my actual involvements with others in the world. . . . It is not assured once and for all, for it is our response to the need of others to grow which gives us place.[14]

Caring and place are so intimately interdependent that they offer the means that most small churches use to involve their congregations in community caring and Christian witness. These program themes will be examined further in chapter 6.

(2) Social space implies an intimacy that is more than many people want or need. Members of small congregations handle intimacy differently. Some members enjoy the contact, the support, and the flow of information. One pastor complained: "I serve the best community grapevine in the county—but they never produce anything but juicy stories. Why don't they talk about something important?" They do: they talk about people.

Other members react to intimacy with a kind of formality, even toward those who have been well known to them from childhood. For example, one pastor in the Midwest told of being introduced by the clerk of the congregation to one of the leading citizens of the town, each addressing the other by the title "Mister." Only months later did he discover that they had grown up together, "climbed the same apple trees, and dammed the same streams." Like workmen forced to live together in the wilderness, the two old friends had assumed a posture of distance to protect themselves from too much intimacy.

A third way of handling intimacy is through aggression. If too many people are too closely pressed, a certain amount of hostility defines the internal boundaries and clears the air for continued socializing. Some of the conflict has become stylized and socially tolerable, but some is personally and socially destructive. We shall consider these questions in chapter 8.

(3) Social space provides a cocoon in which significant experiences can be remembered and replayed. In congregations where personal relationships are primary, there develops a stabilizing sense of timing, noticeable in the rhythm of the worship hymns and the cyclical events of the changing seasons. This community measures time in terms of significant experiences, and space in terms of the people who share it. This is a relational theology where God makes himself known in people-places, and people-times.

A theology of relationships affirms the past: family, important people, significant events, and "historic" places. The fabric of memories anticipates perpetuity. Perhaps the individual will be gone, but the congregation will remain. In this context, mere temporal problems seem insignificant. When confronted with a budget that could not be balanced, the church treasurer simply nodded, saying, "Yes, hmm." There was no solution immediately available, no suggestion for dealing with the problem, no expectation that a resolution would be found soon, if ever. Neither was there any hint of resignation or thought of closing. The theological implications of social place will be considered in Part 2.

(4) Social space is hard to enter. When the members are asked why they belong, they usually do not single out the pastor or the program. More often they remember a time when they were in need and the church "saw us through the crisis." When we draw the lines of care between members, we often have an image of a many-pointed star. When we try to lay hold of the caring cell, it often feels like a

"prickly ball" of Christian love. The members' experiences
have bound them together, but also separated them from
the rest of the world. Like all primary groups, the caring cell
is hard to enter.

One pastor and his wife visited a Reformed congregation
with roots in Eastern Europe and were warmly received
before the worship. They looked forward to the communion, since the elements were homemade bread and wine.
But when the worship began, "everything was conducted
in the native language, the prayers, the hymns, everything.
It seemed like we were intruders. . . . Even the youth are
beginning to stay away." Entry into such congregations,
even those who speak English, might seem like eating a loaf
of ethnic bread. Its inner texture promises to be sweet and
delicious if we manage to break through the solid crust. This
experience of inner texture and outer toughness is universal
in primary groups. But, as everyone with in-laws knows, it
may take a long time to become one of the family. Those
inside are usually satisfied, but what of the others? The
problem of new members will be the subject of the next
chapter.

Summary of a Caring Cell

Many small churches can be described as caring cells
because of the primary relationships of their members. I do
not presume that the caring cell will explain every variety
of small church, or fit every dimension of church life. For
some congregations it may not fit at all. But I believe
that this description offers a positive and independent
approach for seeing the small church with its strengths and
limitations. This approach offers certain immediate
implications:

(1) Human relationships are primary. These relationships
may become attached to events and to objects in a much
more specific way than in other congregations, which have
diversity of interests and rapid turnover of membership.

(2) Human relationships form a caring cell in which

everyone has a place. Since the absence of a member hurts the sense of belonging, the energies of the congregation can more easily be directed to concerns of physical and mental health. Small congregations are especially sensitive to hospital calling, prayers for healing, and the power of God to make people whole.

(3) The rhythm of the right people in the right place satisfies a human need for order in the ministry of the small church. Orderliness is the skeleton of the caring, Christian congregation. At times, the urge for order and routine seems to dominate over the will to care for people.

(4) Churches develop a character from their unique experiences. When that character is identified, the congregation may be motivated more from a sense of Christian "pride" than from a desire for new accomplishments.

(5) Since people are most important, the caring cell can be aroused to help particular people in need. "When the need is clear, the response is overwhelming," said one appreciative executive.

(6) Finally, many people find a peculiar strength and serenity when they are seated in their place. Pastors who are willing to sit in the pew *with* their people often discover an otherwise unknown array of burdens and an untapped source of spiritual strength. One pastor sat for several minutes in silence with an elderly woman of his congregation. Then he recorded her prayer:

Lord, I'm tired—so very tired. Please, Lord, I don't want any advice. I've heard enough of that over the years. I don't want to be told what I must do. I've been told that often enough. Lord, I just want to sit here in quietness and feel your presence. I want to touch you and to know your touch of refreshment and reassurance. Thank you for this sacred little spot where I have heard your voice and felt your healing touch across the years. Thank you for these dear friends who share this pew with me. Together we have walked the tearlined lanes. We know what it is to be lonely. . . . We also know comfort and strength of one another and the joy of your presence. O God, the child of my womb has become a drunk. . . . Daily I watch her die before my eyes. Where have I failed, O Lord? How can I find the strength to continue? How can I help my dying daughter find herself?

O God, soon I will be going home to be with you and my husband. I am ready, even eager. But until that day help me to be a help to others. Give me strength to live this day and peace to enjoy it. Amen.

He called his experience, including the silence, "listening to the pew speak."

For Further Reading

Berger, Peter L. *A Rumor of Angels.* Garden City, N. Y.: Doubleday, 1969.

Erickson, Theodore H. "New Expectations," in *Small Churches Are Beautiful,* ed. Jackson W. Carroll. New York: Harper, 1977.

Oden, Thomas. *The Intensive Group Experience.* Philadelphia: Westminster Press, 1972.

Olmsted, Michael S. *The Small Group.* New York: Random House, 1959.

Exercise: Gatekeepers and Patriarchs/Matriarchs

In small congregations, several functions are particularly important in helping new members become part of the congregation. Several people may perform these functions; sometimes different people take turns. One function is the gatekeeper,[1] and another is the patriarch or the matriarch. Using the seating sketch from the Choreography of Worship exercise, circle the gatekeeper(s) in green, and star the patriarch(s) and matriarch(s) in yellow. They may be identified as follows:

The *gatekeepers* linger around the edge of the church meetings and congregational worship. They are often older, often male. Although they usually do not have positions of leadership, they enjoy greeting everyone, especially visitors. They like to know everyone and everything, but they avoid being at the center of events. One pastor reports that "during the sermon they go outside, just to talk." They may not agree with what the church is doing, but they enjoy explaining it to others. Gatekeepers will be found near the "gates" of the group. More likely, they will find you.

The *patriarchs* and *matriarchs* are at the center of the church. They sit in the center of the sanctuary, and they feel in the center of the congregation. They may have wealth and be involved in many activities, or they may have passed their prime. They may be friendly or aloof. One pastor describes a matriarch as "gruff on the outside, but a very caring person." They may no longer sit on the official boards of the church. But they have one essential feature: Patriarchs and matriarchs have lived through the historical moments of the church. In their presence they carry the identity of the church. They remember when things were different, and "how we got to where we are."

Chapter Three

Growth by Adoption

How can a small church grow? This puzzle lies at the heart of the small church problem. There are four answers to this question. They are in apparent contradiction. Yet, for most small churches, the same four answers should be given despite their apparent discrepancy:

This small church has grown.

This small church can't grow.

This church could give up its smallness and change into a larger congregation.

This church can absorb new members without growth pains.

The Small Church Has Grown

Most small churches have already grown much bigger than they "ought to be." They look small only when compared with the larger organizational churches that flourish in metropolitan communities. If we define the church by the business *B*s of religious institutions— budgets, buildings, and bodies—the small church comes out on the short end. But the small church appears much stronger when measured by human relationships. If the church is defined by the number of people who know and care about one another, by name, then the small church has already grown.

The genius of the small church is that everyone knows, or knows about, everyone else. In the small church everyone has a place. Everyone has a place to sit and a place in the social fabric of the congregation. In larger congregations, the subgroups are considerably smaller than the whole congregation of a small church: a fellowship group may have thirty or forty members; a committee or a study group may have fifteen or twenty participants; a prayer cell or a sharing group may not tolerate more than eight or ten people. In larger congregations, members may know persons in one or more other groups. In the small church, *everyone* knows, or knows about, one another.

The small church is a single cell of caring Christians. The membership may be only one hundred people, or even fewer. But the network of people who care for one another may be much greater. A better measure might be the number of people who turn to the pastor in time of need, or who support the church at Christmas, Easter, and the annual pancake festival. If the church has a long association with a piece of land and a particular cultural heritage, it may embrace two hundred, perhaps three hundred or more people who know each other personally, by family, name, and place in the community.

The small church has grown. If measured by the impact of the church upon the relationships of its members, many small churches are already much larger than their more "successful" suburban sisters. Churches with larger memberships are simply collections of several smaller groups. In small churches, more people know more people, and know more about more people, than in most larger congregations. In the relationships among people, the small, single-cell church is much larger than any one cell in the larger congregations. When compared to other kinds of caring groups, the small church is much larger than it "ought to be."

When church size is measured by human relationships, the small church is the largest expression of the Christian faith!

The Small Church Can't Grow

The small church can't grow, but not for the reasons that the church itself usually advances and not for the limitations often whispered by denominational committees. Church members usually claim that they would like for their churches to grow. Most church leaders say they would willingly give up some of their many hats of leadership. At times they note the lack of growth potential in the community. More often they are simply baffled by the absence of new members, when the church seems so satisfying to the members who already belong.

Outsiders, and some insiders, whisper uncomplimentary reasons why they believe that small churches can't grow. They say that they are lazy, and small in vision. They note the lack of a "full church program," and urge the addition of particular activities to attract new members. Sometimes they identify the problem with a style of leadership, or the motives of particular people: the officers are afraid of losing their position, or the congregation is "allergic" to new faces.

In their classic study, *Small Town in Mass Society,* Arthur Vidich and Joseph Bensman point out the limited prospects for membership growth in a relatively stable community.[2] They designate two sorts of adults who are not church members (the majority of the community): the first are the people "who look like good prospects, but don't respond," and the others are people whose life-style does not attract the invitation to join. In short, they are the intransigents and the untouchables, which is not a very promising choice.

But the basic obstacle to growth lies in the satisfactions of the present church membership. When the church is seen as one caring cell, the problem is neither complex nor judgmental. The small church is already the right size for everyone to know, or know about, everyone else. This intimacy is not an accident. The essential character of the small church is this capacity to care about people personally. The small church cannot grow in membership size without giving up its most precious appeal, its intimacy.

Small-church members unconsciously feel that they cannot absorb new members without changing the fabric of the group. According to the experts in group relations, the small church is already much larger than similar kinds of caring groups.[3] Members often feel the strain. They feel that they cannot receive new members without losing touch with those whom they already know. They cannot make a radical change in the size of the church without losing their motivation for belonging. In the number of people whom they can embrace in Christian care, the members feel, often unconsciously, that they have reached their limit. They cannot grow because, in a word, they feel "stuffed."

"In many cases the church itself knows that to be small is better," said a pastor in New England. "The members effectively counteract anything the pastor can do to *make* them grow." They may call in the community, or open the building for service to the neighborhood. But most of the members were initially invited by a friend or relative or someone they are related to on the job. Replacements are received almost naturally, but church *growth* is almost impossible.

The church treasurer spoke to the council: "Yes, money is a problem. If we only had a few more members, we could pay the bills." But growth is more than a problem of managing the numbers. For the sake of the budget, they want more members to share the costs. For the salary of the pastor, they could utilize more steady income. But growth in membership affects their satisfactions in belonging. They have reached the limits of their personal compassion. Small-church members are unwilling to change the nature of personal caring for the goal of financial solvency. The small church can't grow while it remains "our (small) church."

In Christ, members of small churches can love and show concern for all the earth and every living creature on it. But in Christian caring, they have drawn the line. They want to "place" everyone who belongs to "our" church. For the sake of knowing and caring, they have set the limit. Their style is not more or less "Christian." It is a choice they have made, not always consciously.

When an energetic young pastor brought the first five new members into an ethnic congregation of two hundred members, one of the old family members confided, "With so many new faces, I hardly know anyone anymore." She was not unwilling to welcome them. But she knew that "our church" was no longer what it used to be. The small church cannot grow and still remain a small church; it will never be the same. One sensitive urban pastor suggested that the maximum number of new families that the congregation could absorb "could never be more than six or seven each year."

The Small Church Can Change into a Larger Congregation

Rapid membership growth is possible for many small churches. A substantial minority of small churches could double their membership in the next few years. Rapid membership growth depends less on community potential, more on the values and attitudes of church members. Members of the congregation must want to grow so much that they are willing to give up the satisfactions of knowing, or knowing about, *everyone* else in the congregation. They must sacrifice the satisfactions of being a small church.

One ironic twist in this phenomenon of smallness emerged from our review of New Church Development (NCD) projects in the 1960s. In NCD strategy, the mission pastor developed several cell groups of prospective members in homes throughout the community. When a sufficient number of cell groups were organized, the mission pastor tried to unite them to organize a congregation and construct a church building. Some mission pastors were exceptionally gifted in integrating the different cells that had been meeting separately. Other pastors found this process very difficult. The first group of pastors reported their feelings of success in helping the many cells gel into "one big happy family of the church." The second group of pastors worried about their "failure to work out internal differences between the various cell groups." The irony

only emerged later when we discovered that the congregations that gelled quickly ("successfully") frequently
stopped growing. The other congregations, which seemed
to be struggling with their separate, distinctly different
cells, continued to increase in membership. They have paid
off the first mortgage, sometimes two or three more
building mortgages, and are now thriving, "successful"
suburban congregations. They have excellent programs,
with something for everyone.

The difference is very clear. Members of larger,
multicelled churches cannot know each person in the
congregation. They do not expect to know everyone. Larger
churches attract and assimilate members through several
small units that are "hungry" for members to share a
common task. New members do not join the whole church,
but become attached to their group. When a group attracts
so many members that it becomes unwieldy, the group
subdivides to provide space fo more new members. Like
cells of the human body, the church body has *grown by
division* of large cells into two or more smaller cells.

Most membership growth programs have been designed
for large congregations with different groups and diverse
interests. These programs have been particularly effective
in suburban communities where the population is management oriented and highly mobile. Congregations have
taken great pride in a full church program, from preschool
care to programs for the elderly. This program demands a
vast variety of social cells, each receptive to new members to
fill the necessary functions. The more cells, the more
members: the congregation grows by dividing.

Dividing is one activity that the single-cell church refuses
to do. A church program with something for everyone is
unnecessary when everyone shares in whatever happens.
Members are either present or are immediately informed by
the grapevine. Additional church activities are either
exhausting or divisive. Growth by division is subversive to
the essential satisfactions of belonging to the whole church.

The imperative to grow numerically has been stated most

forcefully by the advocates of the Church Growth Movement. C. Peter Wagner writes: "I wish to disassociate myself from the big-church–small-church debate. . . . The optimum size of each church depends primarily on its philosophy of ministry. Churches, much like people, have personalities that set them apart from another." That sounds affirmative, but Wagner continues: "But whether a church is large or small, it should be a growing church. . . . Healthy large churches and healthy small churches are evangelistically effective." He goes on to note the implications: "If smaller churches are growing they eventually will become large churches. Just as every river was once a stream, every large church was once a small church. When this happens, new small churches will continually be needed."[4]

Wagner describes the growing church, with levels of participation. Everyone shares in the large celebration, where anonymity "is not bad at all." A smaller group can be gathered into the congregation, as a "fellowship circle" of about two hundred worshipers. Last, there is the Christian cell, which "is so close to a family situation that I like to call it a 'kinship circle' to contrast it from the membership circle and the fellowship circle."[5]

That's the logic of church growth, and it works. But the small church must be "converted" to believe that the change is worth the cost. One pastor at a conference on methods of evangelism observed that "any of these methods, if used conscientiously, would turn the small church into a large church, and that's the one thing most small congregations don't want to see happen." Members of the small church know the alternatives.

Members who joined large and small churches were compared and interviewed in a careful study by Allan Wicker.[6] Both groups of new members agreed that large churches have better church schools, more formal worship, more efficient committee organization, and so forth. But they also both agreed that in the small congregation, the members spend more time at church, work harder, know

53

the pastor better, and seem to care more. Each group separately seemed more satisfied with the choice that they had made in the church that they had joined.

In a small church, membership growth means a loss of contact with the whole body of the congregation. The members must give up knowing everyone, for the sake of sharing with many more people whom they can never know. Even when members have agreed to try to get their church to grow, they often find that the heart resists.

Pastors who encourage the small church to break into several separate activity groups have received a variety of nonrational responses. Some pastors report that members "agree with the programs," but become irritated over petty things "that never bothered anyone before." When one pastor encouraged a series of home meetings to help new members become acquainted, he was accused of "breaking up the church into pieces." In a literal way, he was: the church grew in membership. When another pastor suggested the need for two, somewhat different Sunday worship services, he was warned that it would "divide the congregation." It did just that: the tension diminished, and each service group prospered for a time. When the community has growth potential, any congregation can grow—if the members are willing to let go of their satisfactions in being close to one another. Some small churches are "converted" to larger congregations, with a full program and something for everyone. But they are not small churches anymore.

New Members Without Growth Pains

Most small churches will not experience the rapid growth in membership necessary to become larger congregations. Yet they can absorb new members into the existing fabric of the congregation. Even in situations where there appears to be no significant membership potential in the community, small churches can still be more effective in bringing a few "intransigents" into the church family. In other communities, where churches are rapidly expanding their membership, some congregations may feel called to remain relatively small as a single-cell congregation. New members can be absorbed without the pain of radical membership dislocation.

The small, caring, one-cell church behaves like an extended family in many ways. There are levels of participation, and a latitude for individual characters. Members contribute to the whole, yet have a life apart from it. The most natural form of growth for a small church is the way a family grows, by birth and by adoption. Unfortunately, young people who have been born into the small church often leave the community when they become young adults. Some young people will return; many will not.

Adoption is the other way for families to grow naturally. Adoption is a biblical metaphor to describe the way the outsider becomes part of the family of God. According to the Apostle Paul, in his epistles to the Romans (chapter 8) and to the Galatians (chapter 4), we are adopted into God's family through the witness of the Holy Spirit. We were not family, but now we are. The metaphor has already been absorbed into Pauline theology when it is mentioned only in passing in the letter to the Ephesians (chapter 1). Although Paul is most explicit, the process of adoption by God is implied also in the Synoptic Gospels, in John, Hebrews, and Revelation.

By adoption, the newcomer joins the history of the family. However, he or she cannot make a unilateral decision to join. Newcomers cannot work their way into the family, to achieve belonging. In the same way, membership in the small church is a shared experience, based on a common faith and mutual understandings. The faith-statement of the new member must be mingled with the story-history of the congregation. The adopted member of the church must learn to appreciate the artifacts and traditions of the family, the annual feasts and perennial threats, and the "family secrets" of their history. It takes time to adopt a child. The whole family/church must participate.

The adopted member looks in the opposite direction from those who join the small task group of a larger congregation. When new members join a large-church activity, they accept a common goal that holds that group together. In such activity groups, the new member often shares in defining and creating the common future. But adoption looks in the other direction, not to the future but to the past. The new member is adopted into the family history. The adoptee must absorb the values of the church, just as the church absorbs the new member. Interesting characters, like patriarchs and gatekeepers, make adoption happen more easily.

Gatekeepers and Patriarchs/Matriarchs

In the exercise at the beginning of this chapter gatekeepers and patriarch/matriarchs may seem irrelevant to the work of the church. Gatekeepers are often seen as busybodies because they want to know everything but take so little intiative in personal leadership. Matriarchs and patriarchs are often difficult to work with, especially in the introduction of new programs. To the young pastor they may seem irascible antiquarians.

But in the process of adoption, the functions of gatekeepers and patriarchs/matriarchs are essential. Gatekeepers are the matchmakers at the door, or keep a watchful eye from the choir loft. They may not embody the values of the church or carry the weight of leadership. But they are gifted with the pleasure of communication—gab. They like to talk to anyone, especially to visitors. The gatekeepers interpret the church to prospective members, sometimes with a glad hand; but at other times they lock the doors. If the gatekeepers like the match of church and visitor, adoption is possible.

Matriarchs and patriarchs are the informal officers who

accept the new members into the family. They complete the process of adoption by sharing the church history with the new members. New members know they are accepted when they have heard the stories from the elders of the church family. New members do not really belong until they have appreciated the stories and accepted the "old folks" who shared them. When that time comes, the family covenant is completed.[7]

Gatekeepers and matriarchs/patriarchs are not the only personalities who keep the small church lively. The reader may wish to look again at the Choreography of Worship diagram to identify the contributions of many who participate in the small church. In a larger congregation, the Sunday celebration may be more private and reflective. But in the small church, everyone has a part to play. In most small churches there is the Storyteller, the living historian who may embellish for the pleasure of the listeners (who usually have heard it all before). Another common figure is the First Sergeant of the Lord. He makes it clear that he (or she) is not really in charge, but the one who is in charge is "not immediately available." In the interim, the Sergeant makes decisions "according to policy." Mr. Executive Order he was nicknamed in one congregation. The small church has a way of enhancing and enjoying its characters. Readers might identify other characters, such as the Early Bird, the Scorekeeper, the Sparkplug, the Peacemaker, the Bellringer, and others. Small churches have a way of producing characters, or perhaps they are simply more visible.

Reservations and Possibilities

Most congregations cannot adopt members until they take pride in their own congregation's "story of Christian witness." Much of the friction between old and new members revolves around the private ways in which that history is remembered and the in-group process by which it is shared. Some congregations have facilitated the adoption of new members by asking the oldest (and most liberated) members of the congregation to recall and share—as in the Jewish Passover the oldest person answers the questions of the youngest child. A communicants' class in the evening with church officers, storytellers and matriarchs, surrounded by food, photo slides, family albums, and other artifacts, can bring out much of the informal history of the church.

Adoption should be a part of church growth, but not the alternative or substitute for other appropriate programs. The purpose of "adoption" is to help the pride in a congregation's Christian record become the common property of the congregation, not the private possession of a few. The process of adoption can be just as important for integrating new leadership into the official boards of the church, or even for the entry of a pastor into the life of the congregation.

Adoption is a serious problem in many congregations where new members are kept on the fringes for several years, or even longer. We should not cheapen the meaning of belonging by trying to rush it, nor should we use adoption as a mask for unchristian snobbishness. On the one hand there is a need to share our separate histories and common experiences. On the other hand, we have a need to confront one another honestly, in love.[8]

Adoption can have its humorous aspect. One inner-city congregation found itself with a handful of elderly members in a culturally changing community. They determined that their ministry was terminal and that the time had come to "retire the church." Since most had reached the age of retirement, they decided that the church retirement should be fun, that they should do those little things they had always wanted to do together but had been too busy bringing in the kingdom. The church gave up their regular program and began a Tuesday afternoon Fun Time. They sang old hymns and prayed together; they read the

Bible and had a time of sharing. Sharing time spilled over into a potpourri of quilting, quiet games, old records, a little cooking, and whatever they wanted. They dragged all kinds of old stuff from the closets and cluttered up the social hall with memorabilia. To their surprise, they were discovered by the community. Older couples and elderly people living alone began drifting in on Tuesday, though they would never come on Sunday. The church became crowded and expanded the program. In their retirement, they discovered a booming ministry. When they tried to live out the past, they discovered a new future.

Adoption is a form of "grandparenting," the rediscovery of three generations in families that are far too separated to know more than two generations. Most churches have some semblance of three generations, but usually not in the same families. When new members join by adoption, there comes that happy discovery that the past is important and that the future generation does care—for the person if not for details of the distant event. A pastor reported such an event when his new-member class joined the officers for a retreat prior to confirmation. One fragment of the conversation ran as follows. Youth: "What was the church like when you joined?" Elderly church officer, thoughtfully: "Just the same." Silence. Youth: "Has the world changed since then?" Then came the stories of the first time the old man saw an automobile, that "infernal combustion engine," and his own youthful aspiration to be an ostrich farmer. . . It went for the whole weekend. And it continues several years later. The pastor noted that "grandparenting has a way of happening. . . ."

For Further Reading

Greeley, Andrew M. *Why Can't They Be Like Us?* New York: Dutton, 1975.

Vidich, Arthur, and Bensman, Joseph. *Small Town in Mass Society.* Princeton: Princeton University Press, 1968.

Wagner, C. Peter. *Your Church Can Grow.* Glendale: Regal Books, 1976.

Westerhoff III, John H., and Neville, Gwen Kennedy. *Generation to Generation.* Philadelphia: Pilgrim Press, 1974.

Chapter Four

Exercise: The Pastor's Study and Professional Feelings

The pastor's study is an expression of his or her professional self. In small congregations, the study might be slightly less accessible to members. The study is more likely to be a room in the manse, or in a yoked parish to be located in only one of the "other" churches. But many members have visited the pastor's study. Their impressions are an important way to understand who the pastor believes himself or herself to be. In the context of this work space, we want to know the pastor's feelings about his or her professional ministry.

(1) *The Pastor's Study:* Diagram to approximate scale the pastor's study as you remember it. Include all furniture: desk, chairs, lamp, files, mimeograph machine, bookshelves, and so on. Include all materials, such as books, magazines, papers, program materials, and note items that have particular significance in the life of the church. Include pictures, wall hangings, decorations, table mementoes, and other items of professional and personal meaning. Note where people sit while visiting the study.

(2) *Professional Feelings:* List at least three satisfactions and at least three frustrations that the pastor feels in his ministry and life with this congregation. If you are a pastor, list for yourself. If you are a member, list the way you think the pastor feels.

Chapter Four

Pastor/People Tensions

If small churches are such a caring cell, then why is there
so much tension between pastor and people? As one family
said of the old family leadership, "There's a lot of
management in our small congregation, and most of it
seems to be aimed at keeping the pastor under control."
One sweet, caring deacon asked me to help her understand
"why our pastor always seems to be in a hurry." One
pastor's wife said, "There is a lot of caring in our church,
especially for us. But sometimes too much caring will kill
you."

Human relationships are the stuff that hold the small,
caring cell together. Sometimes these relationships, like
marriage, are deeply satisfying, with time to experience
them together. But not all the members can tolerate
closeness for long periods of time (sometimes for years, or
decades, or generations). Sometimes small churches, like
big ones, get sick. Sometimes the intimacy of knowing
everyone sours into pettiness, nastiness, and abiding
mutual dislike. In larger congregations, people can avoid
one another and still participate in the life of the church. In
small congregations they are still part of the caring cell, even
if they stay home. Even in the most acid relationships,
human contact is not broken. "We do not forget to dislike
them," is the attitude that many members express.[1]

Pastors use a variety of methods to deal with the intimacy
of the caring cell. In a larger congregation, the pastor may
deal with members in a more professional role: church
meetings, hospital calls, possibly scheduled home visits. In
a small church, the pastor has more contact with more
dimensions of the members' lives. At the same time, the
members and the whole community may know more about

the pastor and his or her family life, even in the city. This personal dimension to the professional ministry is basic to pastor/people tensions. In order of frequency, the sources of tension revolve around finance, program development, and the professional self-image of the pastor.

Finances

Money is a sensitive issue in most small congregations. They are always in need, often just surviving. In later chapters we consider ways of expanding congregational resources. Here we note that financial problems affect the pastor/people relationship directly and continually.

Because the church income is relatively low, clergy compensation is often the most that the church can offer and the least that the pastor can live on. As a result, small-church clergy tend to be younger or older than the average pastor.[2] For many young pastors, the small church is viewed as a stepping stone. Some congregations even pride themselves on "the young clergy we have groomed." They are important people, but they do not stay very long.

Clergy provide leadership for the congregation, but usually they do not become part of the community in the same way as others, who expect to remain. "Neither his congregation nor the community regards him as a permanent resident," report Vidich and Bensman. "Though the minister lives and acts within the community, his stable referent group lies elsewhere."[3] The clergyperson is often born elsewhere, has a uniquely different education, depends on regional denominational leadership for recognition and advancement, and personally maintains a system of values not completely in harmony with those of the congregation. One pastor said his worst frustration was the "pastor-member gap in seeing the church and the world. . . . The members are frustrated, and so am I." As perceptions differ and frustrations mount, pastors are increasingly apt to seek friendship and support outside of the caring cell of congregational activities.

In the face of all these differences, many pastors are still warmly welcomed by the members of the small church. But the cycle of pastors coming and going leaves a residue of ambivalent feelings. If the pastor's first sermon is too good, the members begin to fear that "he will not be here very long." If he has the empathy to become part of the caring cell, the members will barter in gifts what they cannot pay in money. The pastor's family will be "treated special." But the final irony is this: If the pastor stays longer than the congregation anticipated, then some members begin to wonder if they have "overestimated our pastor." There grows a shadow of doubt about the pastor's real competence, which can only be dispelled with the rumor that, in fact, the pastor has "turned down several offers in order to stay with us."

On the other side, the pastor personally has another kind of ambivalence about money. Most pastors have unresolved feelings about their compensation: On the one hand, it costs money to live; and on the other hand, they have received a Christian calling. Many small church pastors have a need for modest salary increases. Yet they feel unable to raise the subject directly with the officers or the congregation. Many pastors leave small churches with the impression of a rift between pastor and people, when the real gap was a conflict within the pastor—between the desire to serve the Lord, and the need for a modest income.

Two power figures appear important in this drama: the pastor's spouse (especially the wife) and the church treasurer. The wives of small-church pastors are not more frequently employed than the wives of other pastors, but the motivation is different: wives of small-church pastors are more often employed because of insufficient income to meet family expenses.[4] Further, because of their own professional training, the wives of rural pastors often feel that there is no appropriate place of employment that equals their qualifications. In an urban or rural setting, if the spouse has satisfactory employment, the pastor may extend his stay in the community. If not, he may leave sooner. In general, the spouse's job satisfaction appears to be more important than the pastor's evaluation of his or her church ministry. This marks a dramatic shift in the pastor's sense of mutual calling, which has taken effect in the past decade.

The treasurer is the other figure who often uses his position dramatically to affect the length and effectiveness of a pastorate. "Because of the [congregation's] uncertainty of income and the continual need to scrounge in order to survive, the treasurer often develops a conservative/protective stance which quenches any enthusiasm for new programs."[5] Whether the treasurer represents a power figure who needs to control, or a more flexible leader who "yearns to make a change if the entire congregation will help by removing the loneliness of his responsibility,"[6] the pastor cannot resolve the conflict without involving more people from the congregation. Only an active membership can liberate an oppressed treasurer.

Program

Program "success" is the second most frequently mentioned source of tension between pastor and people of the small church. This frustration is exhibited at several levels.

Pastors often express frustration at the number of people who are available to participate in any particular program. There is a "critical mass" of assembled people necessary for a program to feel "right" to the participants. There may not be enough women available for an association, or youth for a commmunicants class, or toddlers for a church-hour nursery.

Even if the participants could be found, pastors often feel that their churches lack the adults with proper training for leadership positions. "How can we have a Sunday school," laments one pastor, "when we don't have any teachers?" Even with training, the teachers would be faced with materials designed for many small groups of homogeneous participants. Pastors usually have had their student training in larger churches, and lay leaders tend to be home grown. Too often, the members feel inadequate and the pastor feels unappreciated.

Different measurements for the "success" of the program lie at the heart of the conflict. Denominational reports tend to identify success with numbers. Defining "church" by the number of members is only the most obvious pressure. The numerical inquiries seem endless: such as number of worshipers? number of church-school classes, students, teachers? number of pledging units? total income, special income, benevolence income? number of baptized babies, adults, communicants? number of marriages and funerals? In addition, there are the more subtle questions about programs, condensed into numbers: how many church groups? what kinds? who comes? using what materials? with what income and expense? The message is clear: the effective church is program, program, and more program. The church may not be simply the number of people who attend on Sunday morning; but it is the sum of all its parts, the total of all its different activities. The pastor is a program pusher, hustler, huckster. The "real" church has something for everyone. That is the denominational message of success.

But a small, caring, single-cell church has a different definition for success. For a real program, everyone is present. An almost real program may not be attended by everyone, but all who are absent will hear about it before nightfall. When everyone comes to everything, pastors do not need to plan and push something different for each age group and interest center in the church. Such program divisions are seen as divisive by members of the caring cell. Alan Waltz observes, "The local congregations, especially those smaller units . . . have been asked to work in organizational settings which were not of their making, to their liking or suitable to their needs."[7]

These conflicting definitions of success precipitate three kinds of problems for pastors of small churches: financial resources, human resources, and exhaustion. First, programs need money to support them, and materials to work with. There is a cost to the church whenever the building is opened. There is a cost to the membership when trips are organized and materials are ordered. An energetic pastor may add as much as 10 percent to the cost of operating the church simply by promoting his well-meaning programs. When the treasurer asks about the source of funding for these programs, pastors sometimes feel that their leadership is being threatened. Program ideas become very personal. As one pastor complained when his hot-meals program was challenged on the grounds of fiscal feasibility, "They just didn't like my 'baby.'"

Second, beyond the tangible, financial resources, new programs also require an investment of human energy. Many times the new pastor will feel the need for new programs simply to prove that the church is alive. Old members of the congregation may not feel the same urgency to prove their existence. One such pastor exploded at his official board: "Why do you vote for programs that you do not expect to personally support?" He accused them of apathy and hypocrisy, in the name of Jesus. Later one board member took him aside quietly and asked, "Is it hypocrisy or apathy, or is it Christian kindness to give you the permission to do what you have the desire and the energy to attempt? We were only trying to be helpful."

Finally, when the tangible and human resources are expended, exhaustion follows. Sometimes effective leadership can inspire a flurry of activity. In a patient, loving way, many small churches have responded to the leadership of pastors who have called for a rich diversity of programs with something for everyone. They did it all. But when the young pastor receives the inevitable higher call to a place of greater responsibilities, they are exhausted. A time of quietness often follows a season of feverish activity.

One denominational executive who helps small churches in their search for pastors has become particularly sensitive to symptoms of exhaustion. He claims that he can predict the length of time a small congregation will take before they call the next pastor. He has calculated that the time between pastorates is directly related to the number of programs that the last pastor initiated: the more programs, the longer the interval. "The small church needs time for R & R, rest and recovery," he says. "They may not even assemble a pastor-nominating committee for a year or so, until the people are rested and ready." They are, says one observer, "burned out."

Small church programs can be enthusiastic and effective. But the programs must fit the style and character of the congregation. The importance of "place" in the organization of the small church has been underscored by the work of James M. Palmer. In a study of rural churches in Alabama, Palmer noted that smaller congregations had more "groups, positions and actors" than the larger congregations, up to the size "beyond which it would be impossible for everyone to be personally acquainted with every other member."[8] Organizationally, the small church provided a place for everyone and felt good when everyone was in place.

Some pastors seem to tune in more easily to the pace of the small congregation, with the rhythm of changing seasons and time for the needs of people. One Ohio pastor responded to a discussion of time in the pastorate by saying he was glad to have found the small-church ministry after serving in larger churches: "One of the things I like best is the pace. People don't look at their watches every few minutes during a conversation."

The Self-Image of the Pastor
The Pastor's Study and Professional Feelings

The exercise at the beginning of the chapter provides an opportunity for pastors and members to "see their feelings" and examine the professional images that they project. Usually, the diagram of the pastor's study will suggest the ambivalence of our Christian calling: it is a personal work space, but it is also an arena to share with other people.

Usually the pastor is surrounded by materials that support the program of the church: the desk, the bulletin board, the swivel chair, the telephone, perhaps a diploma, endless stacks of papers and program supplies. The pastor is a program pusher, and the study is usually a workshop, a space for constructing programs.

In most pastors' studies, the visitor is kept at a distance. Typically, a large desk separates the pastor and the visitor. But often the barriers are more subtle, such as the size of the books (heavy and "important" looking) or the heights of the chairs (the pastor sits higher) of the glare of lights (the visitor looks toward the window).[9]

Now compare the atmosphere of the work space with the satisfactions and frustrations that the clergy feel in their calling: Most frustrations are related to unfinished work and inadequate programs—interruptions, too much busy work, urgency to produce, disorganization, too much to do and too little time. Like the pastor's study, his or her frustrations reflect the pastor's concern for work to be done and schedules to be met.

Now turn your attention to the pastor's list of satisfactions. Typically, most of the satisfactions are in contrast to all the other impressions. For most small-church pastors, the satisfactions are overwhelmingly in the area of personal relationships. Typical satisfactions include: working with people, sharing lives and crises, feeling loved and supported, preaching and pastoral calls, ministering to people, having a family and sharing family with others, enabling people. Of course, some satisfactions are related to a job well done. Some frustrations include "being too accessible" (too near to people).

But the contrast is consistent and striking: In the first three areas of his or her office life—appearance of the office, the visitor's impression, and professional frustrations—the pastor has a self-image of one who constructs and pushes program. But in the satisfactions of a Christian vocation the small-church pastor feels rewarded by personal relationships.

If that's the reward, then why so many tensions and role conflicts, not only with members, but primarily within the lives of the pastors themselves?[10]

Power in the Small Church

In the small church, many pastors suggest two kinds of problems: they have overrated their power in changing the community and underrated their importance in touching the lives of people.

When disagreeing with a leading member of the congregation, a pastor sometimes really hears the famous line, "Reverend, I was here before you came *(pause)*, and after you are gone, I will still be here." That's the classical definition of the continuity power that holds the fort in many small churches. The pastor enters the situation as "servant of the servants of the Lord." The leadership, which may appear to be apathetic toward outside motivation, has remarkable energy for maintaining the *status quo.* One student intern noted the delights of being "part of the family," but also observed the "fierce loyalty and determination" of their Christian commitment.

The young pastor may confuse high visibility with leadership, the distinction between which Vidich and Bensman make very clear.[11] The pastor is middle management. He or she does not own the store but only manages it. Both the pastor and the congregation know that the store really belongs to the Lord, but the fabric of the congregation knows who owns the voting shares in the corporation. The small-church pastor is a manager. (The same is true of the large-church pastor, but in more structured organizations the flow of decision-making is more obvious and more "rationalized.") Power may have gravitated to the treasurer, or to the first sergeant of the Lord, or to the matriarch. Power may still be widely distributed among several families and significant people in the congregation. Power does not have to be on the church board, vestry, or council. As long as the pastor runs the store according to the established policies, power figures are willing to remain out of sight.[12]

Power in the small congregation will surface only if the established procedures have been threatened or community values have been challenged. Management questions will be considered in chapter 8. Here we note that a misunderstanding of power has created many difficult tensions between pastors and people in small churches. In many small churches, the pastor is a gatekeeper, unless and until he or she becomes a lover.

The Lover

Professional distance is a source of tension in many small churches. Members of small congregations want the benefit of skilled pastors to serve their churches. But even more important, they want someone whom they feel they can know personally. The most frequent personal frustration for the laity is the feeling that the pastor, hiding behind that professional polish, is not a real person. They want to know the person; that is their first priority.

Based on the distance between the pulpit and the pew, three styles of pastoral relationship may be identified: specialist, generalist, and lover. The person serving on the staff of a large congregation must function as a team player, a *specialist*. The same is true for any staff position in the denomination, the military, the hospital, or any other institution. Most advanced training is directed toward the improvement of the specialist's skills in ministry. To the specialist, the personal life and relationships are secondary. The pastor might be friendly or distant; extroverted or withdrawn; married, single, or in transition. The staff member is employed for the particular skills he or she brings to the team.

However, if the congregation has only one professionally prepared person, then the pastor must be a *generalist*. The pastor is a one-person staff. He or she may not do everything equally well, but all dimensions of the organization must be covered. Generalists are measured by the strength of various programs throughout the church.

The small church cannot afford a specialist and is not primarily interested in measuring success based on program activity. The small church is built around the relationships of people to people. They want to know the pastor as a person, first. Only second are they interested in the pastor's skills. Members of the small church want from their pastor what they find most satisfying in belonging to the small church; they are not primarily interested in the specialist or the generalist. The small church wants a *lover.*

The image of lover should imply physical but not sexual connotations. Members of smaller congregations are more apt to be in touch with one another, physically as well as spiritually. The pastor embodies that sense of touching. In some churches, members want to touch the pastor in return. In other congregations it is more reassuring to view the pastor as a loving father figure, austere but available. Whatever the general cultural norms, touching is more readily practiced in small churches. The pastor as lover is a source of stability, a kind of human Blarney Stone. There is no substitute for the presence of the pastor. He or she is the tangible symbol of love, the lover.

Professional skills seem to be a barrier to separate the people from the real person of the pastor.[13] Members of small churches have a curious method of reemphasizing the common humanity of the pastor. They enjoy his or her mistakes. They tell stories about the time the pastor stumbled into the pulpit, or made a slip of the tongue in preaching, or announced the wrong names in the midst of the funeral, or dropped the ring at the wedding, *ad nauseam.* To the educated pastor, who prides himself or herself on polished skills of ministry, these memories are humiliating. To the members, the stories underscore what they find most appealing about the pastor. He or she is a real person. The stories are intended not to criticize the pastor, but to bind pastor to people. Sometimes the pastor will enjoy the stories but the spouse will take offense.[14] The pastor's family who survives will learn that these stories are the lore of the village viewpoint that leads to the deepest kind of human acceptance. Rather than inhibiting the pastor, they are the liberating words that indicate that he or she has been accepted as a person. The pastor is free to be a character in the community.

Few young pastors are sufficiently at ease with themselves to enjoy the "liberation" to be human that the small church provides. Seminary education and denominational placement materials have taught them to value their specific, measurable skills. Evaluation of professional expertise continues throughout the pastor's career. Some small congregations have accepted the special ministry to help seminary graduates prepare for ministry in a very different way. They help them emphasize their humanity, to be pastoral lovers.

But how do you measure a lover? The pastor of a small congregation is often unprepared for the absence of feedback on professional skills, and the avalanche of emotional "stroking." The pastor of the small church cannot use the criteria of success that have been learned from seminary education or found in denominational reports. The small-church pastor has a different set of satisfactions: for example, there are fewer programs, but a higher percentage of the church membership at each. There are fewer people in the congregation, but they can be known (loved) in many more situations. There are fewer comments (or critiques) on the sermon, but more caring for the whole life of the pastor and family. The pastor who wants to keep attention focused only on his or her professional skills will complain that serving a small church "is like living in a fishbowl." The skills of ministry have not shielded the family from the full-time caring, and curiosity, of the congregation.[15] When the pastor's spouse complains that there is no one to talk to, he or she usually means that nothing is confidential in the network of village connections.

The pastor who feels a great need for constant and

consistent measurement of achievements should not expect to find his or her calling to be satisfied by the strokes of a small congregation. But the pastor who finds reward in relationships with people—all sorts of people in all kinds of moods—should find love in the small church, and return love.

As for a sense of achievement: On a Sunday morning when the elderly parishioner who has slept through worship thanks the pastor for the sermon, the pastor of a caring cell will respond appropriately, "I love you, too."

For Further Reading

Carroll, Jackson W., and Fenhagen, James C. "The Ordained Clergy in Small Congregations," in *Small Churches Are Beautiful.* New York: Harper, 1977.

Dittes, James E. *Minister on the Spot.* Philadelphia: United Church Press, 1970.

Glasse, James D. *Putting It Together in the Parish.* Nashville: Abingdon, 1972.

Nouwen, Henri J. M. *Creative Ministry, Beyond Professionalism.* Garden City, N. Y.: Doubleday, 1971.

Pryser, Paul. *The Minister as Diagnostician.* Philadelphia: Westminster Press, 1976.

Part Two: Conserving

"It just feels good to come here," said one elderly member who climbed the steps to the church, leaning on the arm of her middle-aged son. The man turned to his adolescent son and pointed, "I remember when we climbed that old maple tree when I was your age." The boy was not impressed. He whispered to his mother, "Do I have to stay here all day with Dad and Grandma?"

The caring cell of the small church is a natural cocoon for personal memories and shared experiences. For some people the place evokes a feeling, and for others it brings back specific mental images. But for the uninitiated, the place of the caring cell may evoke boredom and frustration.

The richest resource of most small churches lies in the feelings about members now, and the memories of feelings that they have had in the past. Being in the place evokes responses worth remembering. Preserving those memories is important to the small church. Conserving the relationship between people, place, and happening is the contribution of many small churches to the pilgrimage of church members. Small churches are not against change. They simply feel that conserving the past has a priority.

The next three chapters suggest the importance of conserving in the life of most small congregations. They affirm the past as their source of identity in three ways: *Time* is defined by significant events that shape the image and the expectations of the congregation. *Space* becomes place
when experienced with important people who remain as anchors to the past or guides to the future. *Annual events*

and personal passages remind a caring cell of the length and breadth of God's concern throughout their lives and beyond. History is the strength of the small church. Conserving these experiences can provide the motive for continuing ministry and mission.

Chapter Five

Exercise: A Church Shield
or Coat of Arms

The shield or family coat of arms is a symbol of identity that is borrowed from chivalry. The shield evolved with the growth of family consciousness. It first pictured the head of an animal to frighten the enemy and give the warrior courage. The symbols of significant events were added to help the family remember: a tree, a stream, a rock, a fort, or a banner that was captured. When families were joined in marriage and wealth, the shields of the families were joined together. Established families became known by their coats of arms.

Begin by drawing several symbols that seem to suggest the unique character of the congregation. Effective symbols communicate to others without words to explain them. Symbols may be drawn from events in the community or in the church or in your personal pilgrimage of faith. Sometimes an event that happened only once (such as a fire) dominates subsequent history. Sometimes a familiar event happens regularly (such as communion) that reflects the life of the congregation. The exercise should be fun because it evokes the memories of experiences and arouses feelings that many members have in common.

A few symbols that suggest the unique character of your congregation should be selected and shared with a larger group. Sometimes several groups have worked together on the development of the shield, spending weeks or months to find the proper symbols and prepare the geometric designs. The coat of arms can be both artistically attractive and historically satisfying to the congregation.

But begin with a few simple sketches of symbolic events that communicate to the viewer the character of the congregation.

Chapter Five

Memory and Ministry

Belonging Is a Feeling

Belonging to a small church is a feeling. It is based on being among people who know you and among whom you feel at home. Members have lived their faith together. They have celebrated their separate victories and shared their individual losses together in the same place and before the same Father, God. They have learned what to expect from one another, and when to expect it. In effect, if Carol Perkins is late and Sam Riley is loud then all is right with the world, for that's the way they are. People are who they are, although we may not know how to explain it, or even remember to expect it. But Mr. Jones' question about the budget is as predictable as Sue Polokowski's singing off key. "God love 'em, that's the way they are."

The caring church does not treat each person equally. We know one another too well. Each person is accepted, not equally, but individually, by name.[1] Each person has a contribution to make, and needs to be met. The caring church will tend to emphasize the uniqueness of each person.

In the caring community the individual receives his or her name. Naming is formalized in baptism, and remains informal in nicknames. Everyone has a name. People may be known by a skill they display, by an event in their life, or even by a distinguishing physical characteristic. The local merchant who served in the war may be known as "Major" for the rest of his life. The tall boy may grow up with the handle of "Shorty." The old man may still be called "Junior" long after his father has died. The woman who gets divorced may stay divorced in the minds of many long after she has remarried and moved away. People are remembered individually, intimately, sometimes in awkward ways.[2]

Like the love of God in the familiar hymn, the caring cell has a "love that will not let me go." How many young pastors have first discovered the nature of the caring congregation when they tried to clean the rolls of the church? The enthusiastic pastor suggests that the church council adopt objective criteria for membership, such as current participation, or recent contribution, or annual communion. He may even buttress his recommendation with the official documents of the denomination.[3] But before the list of "lost members" has been read very far, the church officers will balk because, "well, things are not really so clear cut." Later, when a removed member reappears, the pastor may have to relive the story of the prodigal son, cast in the part of the angry elder brother. And if the prodigal should die while still "in a far country," the church family may rise up and declare that "he was bone of our bone, and flesh of our flesh—always one of our own."

The small congregation remembers her own. Here they were named before God, and here they will be laid to rest. The significant events in the life of the congregation are recorded "before God and these witnesses," as we remind ourselves in the liturgy for marriage. Here individuals have prayed in times of personal crisis. Collectively, the congregation remembers the experiences that they shared, carefully stored away in memory, like "the afternoon we burned the mortgage," or "those picnics when the church worshiped in the park." Significant people are remembered by the events they shared. Events are dated by the pastor who served—if he or she was more than passing through.

In a personal way, the small church is the place where intimate memories are recalled. A formal church history might be published in a book, with accurate narrative and well-peopled photographs. But each person has an unprinted album of personal memories of church-school classmates and well-intentioned teachers, of prayer groups and mischief, of club meetings, and very private meditations. These memories are not bound by the mind in order of appearance, but they are triggered by clues scattered throughout the building and the people—mingled with memories of "how it used to be here" and the rites of passages for a strange assortment of close friends and distant relations. Worship is a time of remembering, even without consciously considering the past.

In a broader sense, the small church is the carrier of their experience with the Christian culture.[4] The transcendent and eternal God has been felt in this place, among these people. God has touched the members through the moments of celebration, or in the posture of prayer, or through hands that are gentle and arms that hold, in the smells of down-home cooking and the hush of the last to leave. Time is remembered, not as hands of the clock or squares of the calendar: time is remembered as Christian people who cared.[5]

One student pastor in a caring congregation said it very simply with pained honesty: "Small churches look inward, rather than outward. They look backward, rather than forward."

Exceptions to History

History is a strength in most small congregations. They find themselves by looking inward and backward. That statement alone is offensive to some pastors, and inappropriate to some congregations. History is a resource that is not available to many larger and younger congregations. History is rejected as a resource by the theology of some pastors.

Some congregations are newly organized in new and growing communities. They have a future to build on together, but they have no past that is uniquely their own. The innovation and creativity of most young congregations is nourished by the many Christian histories that the members bring from other experiences in the faith. Even they build the new from the old.

Social mobility increases the importance of history, even as it makes a sense of history more difficult. One suburban pastor complained, "I have only been here two years, and we have not been able to grow; but of the two hundred people in my congregation, only forty were members when I came." Such congregations may have difficulty in establishing a firm sense of history. Yet many such areas of high mobility are composed of transients searching for an institution that will offer them a sense of belonging. Mobility may simply speed up the development and turnover of tradition, not deny its importance. "Our contribution," said a pastor in a changing urban area, "is to help people learn that the church was where they were, is where they are, and will be where they are going. They need us to be *here,* before they come and after they go."

When churches move, history may be more of a problem than when people move. When the population moves, the church offers a history in that place. But when the congregation relocates, its history may be out of context. The social history of a congregation may become a barrier for the congregation to reach the community. Some congregations are regional in character (see chapter 9) and draw from a larger area. But neighborhood congregations that move to a new place of worship have the same problems in merging with the community that other churches have in merging with one another.

Some churches, and especially some pastors, deny the theological importance of a congregation's claiming a unique history, or of a person's ever looking back. For some, the rebirth experience in Christ opens the future but closes the past: "He who has put his hand to the plow. . . ." For others the mission of the church is so absorbing that there is no time for yesterday or even today. The strange combination of those who talk about "conversion" and those who focus on "causes" are both fixed on bringing in the kingdom, without thought of the past. But time in the Christian faith is bigger than the future.

Biblical Memory

Our faith is based on memory. When defining the meaning of the faith-experience, or describing the qualities of God, our faith reaches back to the experience of God's people in the biblical record. Israel knows God, because the people remember the great acts of God. "Of these [events], the call and promises to the fathers, the deliverance from slavery and the gift of the land [the conquest] are known from liturgy and confessions to be the key elements of the whole story."[6] The faith of the people is placed in the faithfulness of God. What they remember determines what they believe about the future. What God has done, he will do. "Remember, O Israel, the Lord Thy God, the Lord is One. . . ." Ours is a faith of remembering.

G. Ernest Wright points to the sense of history as being distinctively Christian: Christianity among the religions seems to be the only one that takes history seriously, for it assumes that the knowledge of God is associated with events that really happened in human life.[7] "The biblical point of view was to take history and historical tradition seriously and through them to foresee a future. Faith is thus set within the forms of history."[8]

Above all, Christians remembered. Peter remembered his promises broken and Christ's promises kept. The church remembered the new covenant "in remembrance of him." They remembered the images of the cross in the ground and the stone rolled away from the tomb. They remembered the Resurrection every first day of every week, Sunday. They remembered the gift of the Holy Spirit, and they remembered the words of our Lord. Faith is the memory of those who have proceeded us, the great cloud of witnesses, who walk this way before us. They remembered events:

When Christianity begins to speak of the suffering of God, it speaks of the body language of God's suffering, the cross. When it speaks of deliverance, it speaks of an event, the exodus. Whereas much popular religion is narrowly concerned with *ideas* about God and religion, the Biblical witness remains more concerned with *events* in which the truth is historically embodied.[9]

All Christians share in the biblical memory. History is not just part of our past, but we are part of an unfolding drama of faith. The roots of our Christian experience are a tangled mat of biblical witness and personal experience. Thus Wright calls faith (biblical theology) "confessional recital of the redemptive acts of God in a particular history," where history includes "not only the events of seeming impersonal significance, but also the lives of the individuals who compose it."[10] The story unfolds in the lives of all of us, and in the lives of the congregations where we share and serve the Lord. For some congregations, memory has been their strength and inspiration. For others, the weight of the past has become a millstone and a source of despair. Christian memory can be used or abused.

Abuses of Memory

Many of the negative observations concerning the small church can be traced to bad memory—that is, the abuse of memory—in the caring cell. Old, closed, ingrown, ultra-conservative, prejudiced, independent, disconnected, oligarchical, and hung up on the past are all descriptions that relate to an abuse of history in a congregation. Some history can be a burden, and some can be oppressive. One pastor from New Jersey said: "Our building is not old, it is simply run down. The congregation feels like the church looks—not old, but tired."

Memory can be a burden. The families that once were the strength of the congregation can become its liability. A young pastor in the South commented: "Family hostility blocks communication in our church. Often groups have

rigid lines, and people live separated in their little boxes."
Memories can divide the congregation—who joined under
which pastor. The collective memory of the congregation
can become a barrier to the inclusive church, what Lyle
Schaller has called the "liturgical-ethnic-nationality-
language-cultural-socioeconomic barrier."[11] What is nos-
talgia for some people may be nauseous for others.

Memory can evoke feelings of guilt and grief for the good
old days, especially if the congregation has "deteriorated."
Of course, the good old days may never have been so good
(most sanctuaries reflect the overoptimistic projections of a
growth that never happened). But they are past, and
therefore not as traumatic as the crises of the passing
moment. The older members are aften saddened at the
memories. But the middle generation, the present church
officers, often feel guilty that they cannot equal the feats of
the past—even if conditions have changed. Those who
grieve may be more flexible than those who feel guilty about
the past as compared to the present situation.

Memory can be a means of avoiding the present. Some
small churches have an "edifice complex." The community
has changed, the members have moved away, and the
building is the only familiar landmark left in the community. One consultant told me: "My work with marginal
churches taught me that these Christians have to face a
ministry that is not rooted in the past. . . . We must not
crucify small churches, but we also must not unduly coddle
them."

Memory can be a burden, a source of guilt and sadness,
and a way to avoid the problems of the present. But there
is power in remembering. Memory can stir people
emotionally far deeper than reason will allow. As one
impatient executive observed, "Now that you have
opened Pandora's box [by exploring the histories of
congregations], how can the recollection of personal and
congregational past be harnessed to the ministry of the
present and the mission of the future?"

Uses of Memory

First, memory is the biblical affirmation of what God has done in our lives. We stand in the lineage of our faith when "we remember the Lord's death until he comes again."[12] God has touched us, individually and as his people, through particular people and in particular places. We have experienced the mighty acts of God. In memory we are joined with the whole communion of the saints, past and future.

Second, memory offers us distance from the pressure of any particular moment. In congregations with at least three generations represented (although rarely in the same families), the middle generation usually carries the burden of daily church work and management. They may assume that there is a "right way" to carry certain traditions, and perform certain functions. The older generation has the perspective of memory: they remember that "we did not always do it this way when Mr. Hardy was pastor." Memory liberates through perspective and contrast.

Third, memory offers perspective even on memory. By remembering, we can sort out of our experience what was relevant to that moment and what is of enduring value. Memory allows us to affirm the positive values of caring for people without becoming an advocate for a rural simplicity or an ethnic "old country" that has no basis in current reality. Memory allows us to select from our past that experience which is useful in the present.

Fourth, memory offers images and models of the past that inspire us in the face of immediate problems. The chairperson of the building campaign can remind the congregation of those "twenty-seven courageous founders in faith who first laid the cornerstone for this church." Fund raising, evangelism, social concern, teaching church school—all can be inspired by the memory of those who have "gone on before us," who have "touched us with their love," who have "made this place possible."

Memory is the strongest motive for ministry in the small

cell of caring Christians. Wright suggests that the power of memory is embedded in the gospel story: "An integral part of the proclamation is the apostles themselves as witnesses of the event, a feature which contains in embryo the later insistence that the ministry is an integral part of the gospel story."[13] As we have been touched, so we feel moved to touch the lives of others.

Conversely, the most offensive insult to most proud congregations is the suggestion that the members have betrayed their heritage. One student intern observed that the strongest motivation in the small church was the "fear of letting the church down." Or for a friend to say, "I never would have thought that [action, or inaction] of *you*," is a criticism that stirs the caring cell to response, sometimes with deep feelings.

For memory is more than a recitation of the past as it really was. What we "choose" to remember may be our deepest longings for what will unfold in the future. Our past is a mixture of dreams and fears, never what it really was. Our memory tells us more about who we are than who we were, more about our hopes and fears for the future than what really happened in the past.

Hope. Hope is the last of the spirits that we almost left in Pandora's box. Hope can be released by the positive memory of the congregation. The storytellers in the congregation are no less important than the planners in shaping the future of the congregation. Churches can attempt only what they can imagine. Memory grows with new experience, and tradition builds on significant events. Storytellers who remember events through the eyes of courage and hope can turn memory into ministry.

From Memory to Ministry

Pace, or timing, is basic to the character of most congregations. For many young pastors, pacing is the most difficult dimension of service in the caring cell. Young pastors have the energy of a sprinter; small congregations often have the grace of a distance runner. The result may be a brief pastorate.

The pace of a caring cell may be heard in the rhythm of the hymns, and the timing of the anthem. It is reflected in the cadence of speech, seen in the ambling of unrushed people, noticed in the time it takes for called meetings to get down to business. It can be measured (if anyone cares) in the length of time after the benediction until the sanctuary is empty (in inverse proportion to the number of worshipers), or the length of time between the arrival of the first pot for the covered-dish supper and the time the evening program begins (if there is one). People-time dominates many small congregations and frustrates many program-time pastors.

In the rhythm of calendar days, Sunday provides a rest beat. Sunday is the sacred hour when the caring cell gathers to reaffirm their faith in God, and their contact with one another. The style, length, content, and choreography of worship all confirm the members' pilgrimage with one another and their contact with the seasons of the earth. Pace is important. As one pastor lamented, "They will remember the length of the sermon much longer and more accurately than they can recall what I said."

The church-school experience is part of the rhythm of the passing seasons. One teacher complained that "the curriculum material is too educational, and not enough Christian." She did not mean that it was too complex, or even too finely graded. She was concerned that the basic, simple values that she communicated to her children were obscured in the many alternative readings of the biblical text. For people-time elicits teachers who are, as one pastor said, "regular, but not committed. They come every week, but they never do any preparation or planning." Church school for the children, summer conferences for the teen-agers, weekend retreats for the officers, and every Sunday for the members—these are the *times* to feel the sustaining love of the eternal God, mediated in particular, memorable *places*.

Church Shield and Coat of Arms

There are many ways by which a congregation can remember and record its important events in people-time. Auburn Theological Seminary has prepared a publication to guide congregations in the preparation of written and pictorial histories.[14] They have many suggestions for the people-conscious historian who will sift through records, letters, diaries, newspapers, hymnals, interviews, and a variety of unwritten resources. Such histories have a positive effect on the young, the elderly, the new members (by adoption into history), and on the general membership. They can be enlivened by tape recordings, photographs, and slide presentations, by congregational worship, and even by a full pageant or historical drama.

The church shield or coat of arms provides easy and immediate access to the people-time of a congregation. It has the limitation of recording only the current church consciousness, whereas the investment into historical materials offers greater depth and perspective. But as a place to begin, the shields are attractive to all age groups, and are a relatively simple means of "seeing our feelings." For the new pastor and the outside consultant, the experience has particular merit.

In drawing congregational shields, pastors and church executives tend to represent the church through basic Christian symbols: they suggest 'faith' through the open Bible, *commitment* through the burning tongues of Pentecost, *service* through the outstretched hand. There is nothing wrong with these symbols of faithfulness. But they are not unique to the character of the particular, local congregation. They are concepts representing theological truths. But they are universal images that could be applied anywhere, to any church.

Members of a congregation tend to be much more particular about the objects they use to carry their message. Their symbols tend to be specific things that the congregation would recognize. Thus the pastors and executives reflect the universal values that they bring to the church, while the members express the more unique character of that particular congregation. Although each needs the other, I suggest that if pastors and executives cannot draw a coat of arms that reflects the history of a particular church, then they do not really know the character of that church. If they do not know the history of the church, then they are outsiders who may not know the church well enough to offer any advice or consultation.

Congregational symbols should suggest where the church has been and what they see themselves doing. An older congregation in a Southern town used the oak as its symbol of a tree planted by the living waters. They used the river as the symbol of their relationship to the social and economic conditions of the town. A suburban youth group used the volleyball to symbolize their fellowship, and the doors of the church to suggest their transitional condition of commitments. In the center was "our cross," the one they had fashioned for themselves. A struggling urban congregation used an anchor cross to suggest the influence of sailors in their community, and the firmness of their faith in the midst of change. But their most attractive symbol was that of an oyster, with its many layers of shell and its pearl beyond price—"the faith," they said, "which will outlive us." One intern pastor from Alaska used the Indian totem, the Native American family tree, transformed into a cross. Like the Celtic cross of the sixth century, it symbolized the absorption of the family, village, and personal experience into the outstretched arms of the faith.

The designing of a coat of arms, or even a full historical research project, would be an act of idle self-importance if it did not serve two purposes. First, these mirrors of our experience should help to the surface our unspoken feelings about church membership and our commitments to the Christian faith. For some the shields have been traumatic, when they began to discover that they were "only a bowling club," or that they "had no ministry to others, none that we could point to."

This Do in
Remembrance of Me

Second, by seeing who we are, in faith, we can better decide who we want to become.

For Further Reading

Auburn Studies in Education. *No Idle Pastime—Guidelines for Projects in Local Church History.* Philadelphia: The Presbyterian Historical Society, 1974.

Eliade, Mircea. *The Sacred and the Profane.* New York: Harper Torchbooks, 1961.

Hillers, Delbert. *Covenant: The History of a Biblical Idea.* Baltimore: Johns Hopkins Press, 1969.

Wright, G. Ernest, and Fuller, Reginald H. *The Book of the Acts of God.* Garden City, N. Y.: Doubleday, 1957.

Chapter Six

Exercise: The Silent History
of the Church

Things accumulate meaning and value as they become associated with important events and significant people in our lives. A "silent history" of the congregation can be developed by identifying and, where possible, assembling the objects that have historical significance.

Begin with the place of worship, the sanctuary. The most obvious objects will be found in or associated with the gathering of the congregation. Some of the most important objects may be unmovable or out of sight.

Next, move through the rooms and grounds of the church in search of things that have meaning to the members. Some things are immediately attractive; others are significant because "it would cause a fight to try to move it or change it."

Further, there are some hidden places to look for the silent history. Church closets are often a gold mine of memorabilia, things that had too much meaning to throw out but are too unkempt to display. Soon they will be simply junk. Sometimes the closets of former pastors and retired church officers will yield a treasure that captures the essence of a particular moment in the history of the congregation. Last, there's the kitchen: some of those old pots and quaint serving dishes have a story to tell.

The silent history can be woven into a historical narrative of the congregation that can fascinate the children and remind the old-timers. Through the silent history the congregation is literally in touch with the past.

Chapter Six

Places of Ministry

Places are important because of the memories we have of the people who have shared them with us, and experiences that return when we remember:

Place is space which has historical meanings, where some things have happened which are now remembered and which provide continuity and identity across generations. Place is space in which important words have been spoken which have established identity, defined vocation, and envisioned destiny. Place is space in which vows have been exchanged, promises have been made, and demands have been issued. Place is indeed a protest against the unpromising pursuit of space. It is a declaration that our humanness cannot be found in escape, detachment, absence of commitment and undefined freedom.[1]

One layperson explained it in particularly dramatic terms, saying, "Places have ghosts of the people who have used them. I can never worship without remembering—or enter the choir room without 'seeing' a welcome face." Most of us, although not so graphic in our imagination, have felt the tug of particular places where we have been touched by others and by the presence of the Lord.

Places become important far beyond their material replacement value. Congregations still meet in dilapidated buildings, sometimes dangerous and even officially condemned. The casual observer must wonder at the rationality of people who cling to the old place, especially when they could move to newer facilities nearby. Commitments to space come not from the mind, but from the heart. The church building may be mortgaged and in need of repairs, but, said an urban pastor, "This place is a landmark in a sea of change, and a source of stability to many who never attend." Even highly mobile Americans carry the memories of precious places wherever they go, eliciting a greater nostalgic need for roots among those who seem to have the least.

Biblical Affirmations

Widely different theological streams are joined at one point: the importance of place in discerning and doing the Word of God. Theologies of liberation, with their emphasis on the need for change, and theologies of conservation, with their assurances of the continuity, both join in their affirmation of a God who speaks to real people in particular places. Paul Tournier has put the case:

How are we to reconcile our need both for a universal and for a personal God?

It seems to me that the Bible gives a clear answer. The God of the Bible is indeed a universal God, but he is a God who nevertheless chooses places in which to reveal himself to men. . . .

He . . . chooses particular meeting-places in order to make contact with men.[2]

The relationship between people and the earth is acknowledged in the description of Creation and gift of the garden of Eden. The call of Abraham and the covenants of Israel with God must be seen in the context of the promised *land*. The covenant at Mt. Sinai provides guidelines for service in the land, promised to the fathers, to be passed on to their children. Early prophets warned about the loss of the land, and later prophets in exile looked forward to the return to the land where God will in fact be king. For Jeremiah, the first symbol of the new covenant was the purchase of land in the face of the enemy. The land where "we have known the Lord" is the foundation of Old Testament faith.

But the land is more than the deserts of Sinai or the cities of Palestine. In the New Testament, the relationship of power and the kingdom are central to the good news of

Jesus. Beyond differences in emphasis and interpretation,[3] the centrality of revelation to particular people in specific places remains. In response to the proclamation and person of Jesus, the cornerstone of faith is the commitment to a particular group in a specific place. Jesus both touched the lives of particular people and challenged the assumptions of wealth and the corruptions of power. His message only had effect when the Spirit moved particular people to share their lives in ministry together. Walter Brueggemann summarizes:

The central (biblical) problem is not emancipation but *rootage,* not meaning but *belonging,* not separation from community but *location* within it, not isolation from others but *placement* deliberately between the generation of promise and fulfillment. The Bible is addressed to the central human problem of homelessness (anomic).[4]

Place in Healing

From seminary I was unprepared for the importance of place in the growth of the believer to become an instrument of God's love. I learned this dimension of faith from a patient parishioner in a time of personal grief. After her husband of forty years had died two months earlier, she had spent a quiet time with her sister in another community. One Sunday she returned, came into the sanctuary late "to avoid too many friends," and found that her pew was occupied by a young couple who had begun to attend in her absence. The following Saturday she came to visit me. As a widow she wanted help with what she called "my sin of idolatry." She went on to explain: "For thirty-eight years I shared *that* pew with my husband. I know it is idolatrous, pastor, but I feel God is closer to me there than anywhere else. There is no place like that pew on earth."

On Saturday we left my study to sit in the pew together, and we were both literally touched by the place. On Sunday she shared it with the young couple, and with their squirming child. She shared the pew and her memories. The young couple "took up residence" just a pew away. They became very close to the older woman and to the ministry of that church.

Her experience provides a model for many small congregations who want to reach out but do not know how. They have a sense of God in a place that is precious to them. But they do not know how to share that experience with others. Many pastors have expressed the dilemma: "My folks are very interested in their own doings. But they couldn't care less about what goes on in the community." A church officer in a farming area said: "All our energy is consumed in surviving. We have nothing left to reach out into the community." For both of these situations, the key to service is found in the importance of place.

The widow used her pew in two ways to reach the pastor and then the young couple. First, she invited them to share it physically, and they sat together. Second, she let its meaning touch them spiritually; she told them the story. Both the pastor and the young couple were changed by the experience. In the act of caring, in sharing her place, the woman found herself healed as well.

Place is important in the caring cell. Here we have been touched, and here we remember. But that place will lose its importance if others are not permitted to share the experience. Ministry through a place will touch people in two directions. It touches those who find a place, as in the case of the pastor and the young couple. It touches those who care, as it did the widow. Paul Tournier, who is a psychotherapist as well as a theologian, says: "The giving of a place to those who have none seems to me to be one way of defining our vocation as healers of persons. As we have seen, one becomes a person only if one really has a place. So in helping our patients to find their places we are helping them to become persons."[5]

Small churches have in abundance the two gifts that Paul Tournier says are essential for healing others: they know who they are, and they have a place to share.

Healing Ministries

Healing ministries can be seen in churches who state their particularity. "We are who we are," they say in effect. "We are the community church," says one suburban pastor, "and we want the community to share our building even if they are not members of the congregation." The emphasis is placed on reaching and serving a particular community, or a particular segment of the urban population. One urban pastor explained: "I emphasize the geographical parish; we are the church of this neighborhood. That reduces the threat of being overwhelmed by confining the size of our concern."

Healing ministries focus on one specific human need. As many pastors noted, "We have learned to personalize the issues." Members respond to help people as people. Usually they do not wait to form a committee and get everything organized. Often they do not trust organization, even if they know the people in the local government bureaucracy or the church denominational hierarchy. Even if such human structures would work, they would not seem to be as much fun. One woman said, "We help first and plan later—if necessary."

Pastors often seem to be attracted to the larger issues and the conceptual questions of social policy. Some pastors put their faith in planned community change. The pulpit is used by some pastors to enunciate these larger questions.

Small-church ministries may accidentally precipitate significant changes in community services. In faith, they may move mountains, or at least nudge the power pyramids of their communities. But social change is not their intention or ambition. They simply care about people.

Two kinds of ministries are most frequently found working in and through small congregations: health care and supplementary foods. Usually as a result of a problem of someone in the church or in their community, a congregation will discover the inadequate care available to anyone who is caught in a crisis. In response, such congregations have begun programs of rehabilitation for addiction to drugs, alcohol, and gambling. They have established mental health clinics and upgraded community services through health fairs. Food pantries often grow from a similar discovery of personal needs. Sometimes they are expanded to more formal projects, such as clothes closets in the community or heifer projects overseas. But the spark is personal, and the human need is physical.

Typical is the experience reported by a small church in Ohio. Through a crisis in one family in the community, members of the church discovered the gaps in the government welfare program. A food pantry was established, but it was quickly wiped out. The pastor reports: "Our church officers had to swallow their pride when it was obvious that the church could not do the job alone. We had to be a stop-gap care-giver. We could not run 'our church program,' but we would have to fit ourselves in with government resources and other churches in our area. The ministry helped nonmembers realize that the church does care for them, not just in proselytizing for rice Christians." But the greatest effect has been upon the church. "Members have lost their preconceived notion of mission and have begun a ministry to those in need—our first unselfconscious mission, and it feels good."

Similar stories could be told of many congregations who have reponded to particular people in need. The needs of senior citizens often attract the attention of the congregation. Churches have developed nutrition programs and meals-on-wheels; they have adopted nursing homes and helped elderly people go shopping. Prayer groups and Bible study often bring the elderly together in otherwise dismal conditions. Sometimes it pays off. At least one congregation has funded their entire social ministry through the semiannual sale of "Handmade Articles and Homemade Goodies" prepared by the elderly for whom the program was developed.

Child care is another concern that has found a place in many small congregations, especially day care, nursery schools, and classes for slow learners. Other churches provide help for youth, for distraught parents, and even for those who want to grow flowers and vegetables in the midst of the city.

"This Is Love—Pass It On"

The fact remains that many small churches do not have any noticeable social ministry. They are concerned only with their own doings. They believe that they have given all their energy for survival, and have nothing left for a social ministry. One church drop-out complained that the church will not last when "the will to survive is more important than its capacity to care for people—that's self-defeating."

What is the difference between those who generate programs of community ministry and those who do not? The difference is not found in the number of members, or any of the resources that can be counted, such as money, or mortgage or the ages of members. The difference lies in the attitude of the members.

Small churches with healing ministries have four attitudes in common:

First, they take a Christian pride in the kind of faith that has been passed on to them. They have been touched by love, and remember how important it was for them. By the grace of God, they feel a special satisfaction in passing that love on to others. The storytellers recount times of crises, and how the congregation came through in the emergencies. Legends about the founders include examples of generous gifts and whispering of secret support for those in special need. Caring for others is considered essential to the character of the congregation.

Second, in specific ministries of healing, they responded to a person in need, not to a community survey. As one analyst observed, "Interest followed action." When the need was evident, the congregation responded. The inclination to respond was supported by the matriarchs and patriarchs, and facilitated by a caring pastor. The pastor cared enough to allow the members to respond. The pastor did not short-circuit the request, and preempt the opportunity for others to respond, but rather found the people who were most interested and the ways that were most helpful.

Third, the people of the congregation showed that they "owned" their space together, not individually.[6] In most cases, they had shared in the maintenance: the youth had painted the community room, the women had stitched the curtains, the men had repaired the concrete walk. The place belonged to everyone for the purpose of sharing, because it was the House of the Lord. Like the land of the biblical promise, it was theirs for service, to pass on.

Fourth, the congregation acknowledged their debt to those who had come before. They appreciated what they had inherited. For older congregations, this appreciation is often associated with objects that had historical meaning. For younger churches, it is often reflected in commitment to the broader programs of the denomination. Churches with a healing ministry usually were the first to say that they were just passing on the love they had received from others.

Silent History

The exercise in silent history is a way to lift up our feelings and acknowledge our debt to those who have preceded us. Assembling and honoring the artifacts of history makes our faith seem tangible, even to the youngest in our Christian family. Faith has always found powerful things through which to focus meaning and pass it on from believer to believer, from one generation to the next. The Lord's Supper uses "things" not as a concession to our humanity, but as an affirmation that God has touched us through the particular and mundane elements of life. The cross has been raised over the centuries as a "thing" that points beyond itself, embracing all people, yet located in a particular time and place.

The silent history does not make the objects holy or sacred in their own right. Like all memorials, the symbolic things that point beyond themselves are a way of showing our appreciation to the sacrifice and contribution of those who have proceeded us. Memorials are not shrines, but simply a way of saying thanks to people who made the present possible.

In silent history most attention usually is given to the things that are associated with people in the sanctuary: the pulpit, the Bible, and the vessels of communion, in that order. Personal relationships are recalled in things that make music—organ, chimes, bells, and piano. Many people also remember the windows, the pews, pastor's chair, and even the lighting of the chandelier. But strangely, few adults have mentioned either the cross or the doors, unless these items are architecturally unique.

Outside the sanctuary, consensus declines rapidly. Often there are pictures and lists of people, framed and well remembered. Pastors' pictures are often treasured, the "gallery of old goats," as one teen-ager fondly noted. There are often specific objects that draw the attention of some: the "gathering oak" tree in the front lawn, the cemetery to the side, the furnace "that we once stoked by hand." Many people mention the wall plaques that specifically say "in appreciation" to unknown members of former generations. The names may not be known, but the sense of "thank you" is widely shared.

Exorcising Places

Silent history is satisfying to prepare and widely appealing in its presentation. But it can do more for a church than merely provide for a museum in the narthex. By honoring our history we can satisfy our need to say thanks to the past. When we have recognized the meaning that some places have for some people, then we can liberate those rooms for other uses.

As long as we ignore the "ghosts" that inhabit particular

rooms in the memories of many members, we will not be permitted to use those rooms for anything that might offend their shadow occupants. The silent history can be expanded to include the stories that the walls could tell. Each room in the church has a history, a narrative of the events that have been sheltered and embraced in that particular place. Old rooms can be exorcised by telling their stories, by respecting the meaningful memories of that room for members of the church. Even better, the meaning of the room can be most fully liberated if an object that symbolizes the events of that place, can be honored in the sight of all. Even the kitchen can be freed of restraints when the ghosts of dedicated service are granted the respect and rest they deserve.

To Make a Memorial

In one sense, all Christians have already shared in the silent history of our faith. Such a recognition of the past is embedded in the liturgy of communion. God has spoken to us in particular places through the love and words of particular people. The places and the people are embedded in our experience and carried with us through the rest of our lives. Raising these particulars up to conscious thanksgiving lies at the center of worship and provides the central theme for the liturgy of the Lord's Supper.

Max Thurian of the Taize Community, in his study entitled *The Eucharist Memorial,* reminds us of the Hebraic roots for the final commandment of Jesus for the Eucharist: "This do in memorial (*anamnesis*) of me" (Luke 22:14-20; I Cor. 11:23-26). Thurian summarizes the liturgical actions expected when we "make a memorial" before the Lord: "To think of something known and past, a material something. . . . To recall man's sin and God covenant. . . . To recall something in favor of someone or against him. . . . To recall or remind God by means of sacrifice."[7]

Silent history is one way to make a memorial before the Lord. In our actions we are thankful for the past, recognize our need for continued care, and restore the sense of using the gifts of God until we, like those who have gone before us, come home.

Some congregations have developed the healing ministries, and others have not. Those congregations who care only for themselves are becoming smaller and smaller. Eventually their place will have no meaning, for they have not shared it with anyone. They will have lost their remembrance. But those who serve others are saved from themselves. They have shared their place, and their history lives on in others. I believe that a church is as large as the lives that are touched through the congregation, by the love of God. Caring is the ultimate measure of a congregation's size. In the eyes of God, some "small" churches are tremendous. God is remembered, and his remembrance is shared.

For Further Reading

Brueggemann, Walter. *The Land.* Philadelphia: Fortress Press, 1977.

Mayeroff, Milton. *On Caring.* New York: Harper, 1971.

Tournier, Paul. *A Place for You.* New York: Harper, 1968.

Westerhoff, John. *Tomorrow's Church.* Waco, Texas: Word, 1976.

Chapter Seven

Exercise: A Calendar of Annual Church Events

"Annual events" are those programs which the church sponsors annually for the whole membership, or permits for a segment of the membership (such as the youth), or promotes as a community-wide activity. Some annual events require a heavy investment of the pastor's time and energy. Some are organized by the church officers. Some are blessed by the official board but supported by the work of another group, such as the women's organization. Some annual events are only tolerated by the officers and face annual opposition by the most recent pastor. They survive, like some couples, without benefit of clergy. Annual events often have the backing of annual leadership and the support of annual members for whom this event is the most significant activity in the church calendar.

The easiest procedure for developing the calendar of annual events is to list the months of the year, then write the events of each season next to the month when it usually happens. Even the smallest congregation can fill out a calendar of annual events. Frequently, smaller churches have more annual events for the whole congregation than meetings for separate groups with their individual interests. Every church has some annual events in the worship and the caring life of the congregation.

After each event, note a few distinguishing differences: Who will get the event organized? Some are official events that have the support of the church board, and others are so traditional that they would happen anyway. Who does the work? For pastors who say that "there is no leadership in this church," this moment is often revealing. Who attends? And who contributes? This is an indication of the historic relationship between church and community.

Chapter Seven

Events Worth Remembering

Identity for a small congregation is usually drawn from common experiences in the past (chapter 5) and focused in a particular place (chapter 6). Identity is maintained in the life of each congregation by the rhythm of events. Some events like the choreography of worship, occur weekly. Other meetings are held monthly for the various groups of the congregation. These continuing experiences are the glue that holds the social cell together. Beyond the flow of activity, the annual events provide the pulse for the life of a much larger community.

Annual events offer an ingenious way for the relatively small caring cell of Christian faith to maintain an important place in the lives of many people who share a common history and a piece of ground. Annual events recall people to be physically present to one another. These gatherings and celebrations reenact the source of their common values, and restate the basis of their common faith. A church will usually have several annual events throughout the year, to be enjoyed at such a pace that the resources of a few key people can be the catalyst for the release of much greater energy, which otherwise would seem dormant or unavailable. Annual events provide for the stewardship of people in the small congregation.

Annual events arouse many different feelings and satisfy many different kinds of needs. For the purpose of discussion, I have divided the events into four areas of satisfaction for the participants. In practice, no such formal distinctions are maintained.

1. Annual events mark the *passage of time,* as the cycle of the seasons and as an affirmation of the caring community. Christmas and Easter are universally significant.

2. Annual events celebrate the *moments of personal transition,* of change for the individual, and renewed acceptance by the larger community. Graduation Sunday and birthday luncheons are examples.

3. Annual events recall the *identity of the particular congregation* because of the experiences the members have shared and the people they care for. Homecomings and cemetery picnics are typical.

4. Annual events invite a *wider segment of the community* to participate and to share in the ministry of the church to that community. The Harvest Bazaar and the Spring Pancake Supper are such events.

A word of caution: No small church has all these kinds of annual events. A single small congregation may host only half a dozen annual events and yet satisfy all four functions in each event. For purposes of discussion, I have used different examples to include more of the diversity of annual events now practiced in churches, and to emphasize their different purposes. I hope to encourage each congregation in the development of a few annual events that are uniquely appropriate to the character and ministry of that congregation.

Passages of Time

Time passes. Annual events mark its passing with the affirmation of a faith that is bigger than we are, and a community of support that will outlast us. Time and space have been "staked out" in the annual event that recalls the past and reassures the believer about the continuity of God's care and community support into the unfolding unknown. Lloyd Warner notes this use of the annual event:

Time . . . is a yearly cycle which tidily begins, contains and completes a unit of duration. Each yearly cycle is related at its two ends. . . . Often a festival marks where one link ends and a new one begins, thus ritualizing the separation of the past from the future time. . . . Enclosed within this system, collective memories of yesterday become a reliable and dependable map for knowing what will happen tomorrow, thus reducing anxiety about the future's uncertainties.[1]

Christmas–New Year is the most universally accepted annual event. One of the events in the Christmas octave usually has the largest attendance in the year. For once, everybody comes. The music reflects the binding of past and present: strength of the old and brightness of new. This is one *time* (event) when the congregation sings. This is often the event when the children enact the faith and so incorporate the meaning of belonging far below the levels of consciousness. The children's pageant, candle-light, carols, and communion are mixed with Sunday school class parties and the trimming of the Christmas tree "the way we always did it."

The formal worship is authorized by the board and clearly managed by the pastor or leading members. But the momentum of the event is much larger than any individual or small, official group. Christmas is the Annual Event, and it will happen according to unwritten tradition.

Christmas–New Year is not the only periodic celebration that marks the passage of time. Westerhoff and Neville have observed that 'summer' "in the United States," has become a form of sacred time based on the institutional shift of public schools, a pattern also established in response to the agricultural economic base in which children were needed as field hands during growing season and harvest time. Now we have two ritually celebrated all-American holidays to mark this shift—Memorial Day to begin and Labor Day to close."[2]

Many congregations have tried to institutionalize annual events that would parallel the "sacred time" of the larger society. They have altered the hour of worship in the summer, combined with other congregations for worship, and joined in ecumenical gatherings to acknowledge a faith that is bigger than each congregation. At the same time they have tried to mark off the summer season, with a transitional event in the spring and an annual rally in the fall.

Some churches have been successful in developing these rhythms. Most have pushed hard and produced little. Professor Neville explains:

In American society we can observe at least three concurrent calendar "years" in progress—that of the school, the church, and the commercial-industrial complex. Each will have its own cycles and rhythms. Each will have activity shifts marked by rituals restating periodically its own group position, beliefs, values, and world view.[3]

There is a fourth calendar that must be observed: sports schedules and seasons mark out important events in the rhythm of the year. Along with the other calendars, we also have high-school sports and Monday night football, local community events and the opening day for hunting and fishing. Sensitive church leaders not only avoid conflicts between calendars but, more important, they use transitional events to celebrate the seasons and integrate our different times into an experience of the whole year.

At the deepest level, annual events do more than block out time—they offer purpose to the group, and meaning to its members. Thus Warner writes: "The yearly story of the life of Christ expresses and evokes some of the deepest and most significant emotions men feel about themselves and the world in which they live. The great drama necessarily releases them from quandaries and dilemmas for which rational and moral values have no answers."[4]

Easter, the celebration of the Resurrection, is the annual event that provides the keystone in the arch of Christian time. Faced with the puzzling fact of personal death, the community affirms its faith in the transcendence of God and the eternal life of the believer. Easter provides what John Westerhoff calls "the primary means of intentional religious education, . . . an opportunity for the community to experience and reflect upon its faith and thereby evolve an integrative set of answers to questions about oneself and the world."[5] The darkness of Maundy Thursday, the stillness of Good Friday, the dawn of Easter Sunday have all been widely used as moments for the most significant annual event for the members of small churches. The time speaks truth to eternal questions.

Personal Transitions

Annual events must reflect and speak to the personal journey of members in the church. Gwen Neville writes: "The ceremonies surrounding the life cycle of individuals are found at those times when the person is in transition from one biological or social state to another. At birth, puberty, marriage, parenthood, menopause, and death, the individual is passing through changes that will effect her or his interaction with other group members."[6]

Some transitional moments are reflected in regularly scheduled annual events. Graduation is a time of passage for the child and youth; commencement marks an end and a beginning. Graduation Sunday may reflect the transitional moment, but often the young people have institutionalized their own annual event to celebrate their passage. Annual trips to the beach and graduation parties without restraining hours are annual events that church officers do not plan, but widely accept, condone, and remember. Birthday luncheons by the women's organization, memorial flowers on a particular Sunday, and lilies at Easter may all mark similar adjustments to the personal transitions that have found a place in the regular life of the congregation.

Most moments of personal transition arrive unannounced and cannot be scheduled on the calendar. But they are among the most significant annual events for the congregation. In faith, the congregation is prepared for these events. They have been anticipated but unscheduled. The life of Jesus reflects "the marks of his own rites of passage, conforming in broad outline to Van Gennep's classical conception of what they are in all societies. They include birth, naming, circumcision, the miraculous events that mark his maturity, the Crucifixion, Resurrection, Ascension."[7] When the time comes for the passages, all other time stops. The larger, extended family will gather from distant parts of the country and will linger enough to get caught up with one another. They will share in the solemn celebration of death, the joy of marriage, anguish of illness, or the cries of new life.

Times of personal transition become instant annual events for that year. They are not exceptions. They are expected in the life of faith, but simply are not on the calendar. Personal transition events should be added to your list of annual events and anticipated in every congregation. They provide three essential functions: First, events of personal transition bring together and identify family ties within the larger community. They offer the first contact for an amazing number of eligible marriage partners, who first met as "a friend of the family."[8] Second, these events bring the family face to face with the deepest questions of transition: death, life, family, and the world beyond. These events are interpreted not only with words, but also by the presence of the larger caring cell.[9] Third, these unscheduled annual events provide contacts with people most likely to respond to the invitation for church membership. They are already self-identified "friends of the family."

Congregational Identity

"I didn't really understand what was happening," the young pastor explained. "In my first year I was advised that 'we've started making plans for the annual homecoming. Is that all right?' Before I could answer—no reply was expected—the elder continued, 'Mr. Walton takes care of the place that night, and his daughter arranges the food,' and so on. I didn't say anything then, and I haven't been asked since. But it is a great occasion, and one of the biggest attendance events of the year. It would be the largest worship if they all came to church, but they don't. The crowd comes after worship, for the social!"

The pastor was describing the most familiar and informal sort of annual event. It can be called the Harvest Dinner or Ladies' Night at the Men's Club or the Men's Dinner at Christmas or the Summer Picnic. Whatever the designation, the result is the same. This is *the time* when everyone knows that everyone else will be there.

Plentiful food, ample time, and old friends are the marks of most annual homecomings. When and how homecomings happen are a logic all their own. Some get attached to the Christmas-tree trimming, and others to the rolling of Easter eggs. We could find no consistency to the style of the homecoming. The uniqueness of the event is matched only by the autonomous character of its leadership. Some leaders are officers of the congregation, and others will not be seen from one year to the next. Some have charts and lists, and others just let it all fall into place. Generally the pastor is not needed to organize or even intrude upon the "planning." One pastor even said, "If I didn't come, they would never miss me." Clearly, the event is given by and for the laity of the church.

So important is this event that it has been permitted into the liturgy of many congregations. In a similar context, Warner notes: "Perhaps one of the most significant changes in the contemporary Protestant church has been the recent introduction of several specifically family days into their sacred calendar—all of them coming from the influence of the laity on the church."[10] Mother's Day has become a time of reunion and renewal in many congregations, combining the affirmations of the extended family and intimate church. Other congregations designate a homecoming Sunday, sometimes even a homecoming weekend. One pastor described it as "well-organized disorder, from the opening prayer to the last piece of chicken." He said, "It lasts all day, but keeps the congregation in an uproar for a month of preparation."

Homecoming events provide a basic beat to the program

of the small congregation. Larger churches can keep many activities and events moving at the same time. The energy of the small church must pulsate. In the annual homecoming, a relatively few people can release the energy of many more people who have shared the place and the love of the congregation. As Christmas–New Year is to the calendar and Easter is to the whole church, so the annual homecoming is a time of unique and personal renewal in the life of the small church. Again, Gwen Neville: "A scattered-and-gathered community is especially useful in a highly mobile society such as ours as a means of identifying the community of [faith] significance."[11]

Identity is often established by the affirmation of a common past. One rural homecoming is called the Cemetery Picnic. It is not a morbid or maudlin event to remember the virtues of ancestors who are buried in the church cemetery. The Cemetery Picnic has utilitarian value by generating the imperative to clean the cemetery and "show our respect for the dead." The picnic, or feast, of many special dishes, is not literally *in* the cemetery, but is held on the grounds of the church. And it may take the whole weekend!

A more lively urban affirmation of ancestry is found in the ethnic congregations that recall the culture of the old country. One Hungarian Reformed congregation will spend months in planning for the annual Festival of the Grapes. Women begin two weeks in advance to prepare the traditional Hungarian foods. To confound the Reformed tradition in America, one observer reports, "There is dancing in the church basement, and the food is accompanied by quantities of wine, beer, and hard liquor, sometimes in staggering amounts."

After visiting many homecoming events in small congregations, and larger churches as well, I believe that this kind of annual event provides a useful index for the future of the church. Some congregations have relatively large numbers of people to return, but I believe that these congregations will die. Some may not have as many, but they will be sustained and might even grow. The difference is not in the numbers of people who return, but in the way that some congregations expand the event to include the new members in their preparations. The event is significant in the identity of the congregation. The new member who has helped in the annual event is really adopted into the family. He has shared the preparation for the family "birthday party" of the congregation.

In a similar way, congregations that invite the community to share in its annual celebration will be twice blessed: the community will be stronger for the presence of the church, and the church will be stronger through its public affirmation. Unfortunately, many such annual homecomings are escapes from the present, with the same old people doing the same old things and complaining about the same old problems. They are, as one member observed, "like having tea in the morgue."

Expanding Ministries

By contrast, some small congregations have found that their most effective annual events revolve around their events that reach out and embrace others in their community. In one church, it happened this way: What was once the Men's Club fish fry to benefit the youth program of the church has been expanded. The Men's Club is defunct, but the whole community joins with the church to raise the funding for the summer program, which the church sponsors for the children of the area.

Another church started an annual Valentine party for older people who lived in a retirement home nearby. The party for the elderly has become so popular that it goes on long after the elderly return to the home. It has become an annual event for the congregation, as well as a high point in the calendar of the retirement home.

Watermelon cuttings in the country and rummage sales in the city (and vice versa) have often been a way of mingling church members and neighbors, providing both with the common cause of developing resources for improving the community. Most of these annual events are hidden under the rubric of "fund raisers." They may raise money, but they accomplish much more. One women's group leader reports that the annual fair is the only event "where most of the members contribute something. All of the work is done by the women of the church, with a little help from a few retired men. The pastors don't even know what's happening."

Sometimes the church leaders get involved in ways that reverse the roles of leadership and make the church more like a family. One teen-ager says she likes best to work on the annual bazaar because "we are one family then. I have even seen the pastor cooking, and the clerk of the council washing dishes."

Healthy churches have developed an identity from annual events that seek to serve in the community. All annual events will not be directed to reach nonmembers. But no church can escape its own self-centered concerns without some organized effort to reach out. Even the church building takes on the meaning of the events that occur there, a significance that is not missed by either the younger members or the families in the neighborhood. John Westerhoff writes:

The church building itself, set in the community, is a "school-house." It reveals its people to themselves, tells them about their beliefs, attitudes, and values. . . . The church is a classroom without walls, offering for people of all ages—especially the impressionable young—a boundless hidden curriculum.[12]

Caring Rhythm

"Just because God makes everything fresh doesn't mean that he throws out the old," explained one church member following a meditation on Revelation 21:5. The rhythm of expected events holds together the people of the small church. The annual events and human transitions provide the high points in the rhythm of events. But the backbone of the caring cell is found in the flow of activities. Weekly and monthly routine happenings hold the core of the congregation together. Like the human body, the small congregation finds its strength in carefully ordered habits that do not require continued examination and do not anticipate radical changes.

The identity of the congregation is reconfirmed in the rhythms of worship. The most militant hymns are metered and transposed into a key that fits the congregation. The most challenging sermons are absorbed into a network of caring people whose identity is found in continuing what they have done before. Change is possible and coping is essential, as we will see in the subsequent chapters. But the reassuring rhythm of the congregation keeps them going.

Regular meetings are part of the pace for the small congregation. The meetings may be called for a variety of purposes, but the regularity of participation provides the basic satisfaction for the membership. Meetings are a way of keeping in touch with those who are present, and keeping up with those who are not there. The meetings may be called for Bible study or fund raising, but people-time remains the dominant item of discussion.

Pastoral calling is another part of the regular identity of the congregation. Some evidence of the pastor's presence personally in the homes of members, or publicly in the mainstream of the community, is often mentioned as a part of the essential satisfactions of belonging in a small congregation.

The Sunday church school in many congregations provides the most important link in the chain of regular events. For some, the church school is even more important than the more formal worship experience. The organizational structure may be elaborate enough to provide a place for everyone (although it may function without regard to who holds which position). The rhythm of the Sunday school may be far more important than the content of the courses. As one forlorn pastor said: "I had to discover that the Sunday school was doing more important things than providing education. It was 'communication central' for the life of our church." The church rescheduled the more formal educational activities so that they would not compete with the caring rhythm of the Sunday school.

"I am fed up with routine," said one pastor. "What's the difference between the church and a social club? Or when the habits get engrained, what's the difference between coming to church and catching the bus to work? It's all routine." Yet the routines of church participation should offer more. They are not simply habits of order and process. These events provide on a regular basis what is available in more dramatic form at the annual events: an opportunity for renewal through contact with the transcendent. As Mircea Eliade says, "The experience of sacred space . . . not only projects a fixed point into the formless fluidity of profane space . . . it also effects a break in the plane, that is, it opens communication between cosmic planes, between earth and heaven."[13] The psalmist calls it the Lord's day in a place of prayer, the first day of the week.

Turf Stewardship

The pulse of regular events in the small congregation provides a natural context for brief reflections on raising funds. In the caring cell, money is like time: it is not evenly distributed. As one treasurer explained: "We have two kinds of money problems, the regular and the emergencies. The emergencies are easy. It's the regular bills that kill us." Small congregations have unique problems with systems for budget planning and financial management. The caring cell does not respond well to every-member canvass, every-member pledging, and year-round budgeting.

The every-member canvass is a problem for the caring cell. It presumes that members know one another, but not too well. The callers should know the family called on by name, but they should not be socially or economically dependent upon them. Of course, in the caring cell, people know one another too well. They must depend upon one another too much. They are too close to press the questions that must be asked, and they know too much to use the pre-printed literature. The whole process feels "canned."

Pledging is also a problem for many caring cells. Pledging assumes that the church members plan what they do with both their time and their money. Pledging is part of budgeting. That is a problem in rural areas, in urban areas, and among the elderly everywhere. Rural communities are often still in economic harmony with the seasons: "What we do not have (yet), we cannot give." Urban minorities are faced with an economic instability that does not know the limitations of the seasons. Older people often live on marginal incomes with the constant threat of financial crises. Pledging is not a natural form of giving for those whose future is so beset with uncertainties.

Budget planning in the small church is often "intuitive," based on the expertise of a treasurer who has practiced for a generation. There is no printed budget and no monthly statements that compare this year with former "year to date" reports. The officers are expected to know these things, and the membership is expected to trust them.

In the small church, the right people "know." They know what people have given, what they will give, and what they are capable of giving. They know what are the church debts, and what are the anticipated expenses. They "know," much as the family store is run from the cashbox and the checking account. In turn, the members know how much they are expected to give. Most small congregations give with amazing accuracy and consistency.

Church finance is not a system of pledging or budgeting. It is a "family process" of expecting and receiving. One pastor says: "In the ten years I have been here, the pledges have never equaled the budget. But the current receipts have more than equaled our needs, at the last minute." Another pastor explains: "The small church can receive a better than average response from its people, because they have a strong sense of loyalty. They know their contribution is important."

Actually, it is not accurate to say that small-church members give more than members of larger congregations. In some churches they do, in some they do not. The difference is simply this: when the need is perceived, the small church will stretch to meet it. The small church will stretch to build or remodel their place, the building. The small church will stretch to have the services of a pastor, shared or full time. The small church will stretch to help people in need. But the members will not give blindly to the church budget. Further, they will not accept a goal that they feel is personally unreachable. In most caring cells, they give what they have been giving, minus just a little "to make sure that I am still needed."

One pastor summarized the dilemma: "We just can't face an every-member canvass. But we have developed a concept of stewardship in response to need, real people-need. That's what works." Healthy congregations know the kind of service that their money provides. "When I first came into the ministry," one pastor recalls, "I would have given the widow back her mite. I would have said, 'It's all right, keep it.' I had to learn to let the congregation care about people as much as I did." Once the congregation discovers the satisfactions of caring, "the money can be raised by a phone call."

In turf stewardship, the caring cell church will take care of her own. Within the life-style of the small congregation, membership giving has increased substantially when the congregation has seen the real need, when they have designed the program themselves, and when they have kept the process very personal. A denominational consultant[14] explains one sort of stewardship program that fits this criteria, and has been used with substantial effectiveness. It is a program that can be home-grown in any congregation. It begins with the assumptions that people know a great deal about one another in the caring cell church, that they see a need in the ministry of the church, and that they are looking for a way to help the congregation meet that need on an increased, financially sustaining basis. Under these conditions, the leaders of several congregations have responded favorably and continuously to a program of "step-up stewardship."

Step-up stewardship expects the officers to divide the congregation according to levels of giving: $1/week, $2/week, $3/week, $4/week, and so on. The number of families at each level is listed (but not the names). To achieve the goal that has been commonly agreed upon, each person (or family) is asked to take one step up to the next level. This is not a pledge and not a percentage-of-income approach. In the caring cell, it is a request that members think of themselves as "one step higher than you were." Within the values of the caring cell church, it works to help the congregation accomplish what they feel needs to be done.

Another means of raising funds is through the annual events. Although this is only a minor portion of the total church budget, annual events can be significant in the total financial needs of the congregation. Further, annual events can confirm the adoption of new members into the church family, and it can attract outsiders into the flow of congregational life.

Most surprisingly, when the congregation associates need with giving, the sense of giving is transformed. Not self-denial and discipline, but satisfaction and pride can dominate the stewardship of the caring cell. Giving can be fun when you know how it helps the place we share, and the life we live together—and beyond.

A Healthy Church

The health of a congregation is difficult to measure, especially when we are more concerned with quality than quantity, with spiritual than with material characteristics. Yet I believe that there are signs of health that we must take seriously. A healthy church will care about the members of that congregation, and respond to their needs. A healthy church will care about the turf, the place, the larger community where God has called it to be. In the act of healing, a healthy church will share its place with those in need. A healthy church will have an identity that is carried in the rhythm and pace of the congregation's life together. The identity they share comes from God, who touches them as a people in a place. Small churches are sick when their members lose the touch of caring for one another, healing in the community, and pacing the power that comes from God. A small church will be healthy first, before it can become effective.

For Further Reading

Mendenhall, George E. *The Tenth Generation.* Baltimore: John Hopkins University Press, 1973.

Nelson, Ellis. *Where Faith Begins.* Richmond: John Knox Press, 1967.

Sheehy, Gail. *Passages—Predictable Crises of Adult Life.* New York: Dutton, 1974, 1976.

Westerhoff, John H. III, and Neville, Gwen Kennedy. *Generation to Generation.* Philadelphia: Pilgrim Press, 1974.

Wilson, Robert L. "Resources of People, Money and Facilities for the Small Congregation" and Jeffery S. Atwater, "Programming in Small Congregations," in *Small Churches Are Beautiful,* ed. Jackson W. Carroll. New York: Harper, 1977.

Part Three: Coping

"Your stuff is poison," one urban pastor told me. "It's only good to appease the gray heads of old churches, and to incite the hotheads of ghetto churches. You tempt a church to wallow in the past and make the pastor like it. Your approach may ease the pain of dying churches, but you have not shown us how to help the church to live!"

The pastor is wrong, in part. Caring and conserving are neglected elements of health in many small churches. These virtues should be placed out front, to be admired and continued. Caring for people and conserving the faith provide the unique dynamics that distinguishes many small congregations. They are Christian virtues that should not play second fiddle to other alternatives.

The pastor is also correct. If we spoke only of caring and conserving, we would be inadequate to the Christian faith, and incomplete in describing the small church. We would have emphasized the past and the personal, but slighted the importance of the present. Faith must use past experience to cope with the present, and to anticipate the future. The small church uses its experience of caring and its style of conserving as an effective means of coping in a changing world.

Coping is a neutral word. Some would have preferred a more aggressive term, such as conquering. Coping carries the connotation of effectively dealing with the difficult, the unexpected, and the mundane. Coping has a quality of stability, if not success. It does not conquer and vanquish the world, but rather endures and lives in coexistence, sometimes in harmony.

Coping is evidenced in three dimensions, which will be considered in the following chapters: (1) Effective small churches have a clarity of purpose that fits with their identity, in the midst of which they can accommodate great conflict. (2) Effective small churches are comfortable with the kind of witness they can make. (3) Effective small churches admit that they are only members of the Body of Christ. With other members of the body they exchange both perspective and resources.

Chapter Eight

Exercise: Church Groups, Goals, and Purposes

This exercise in matching can be most effective when it is attempted individually first, and then the results are pooled.

Draw a line down the center of a working sheet of paper (several sheets may be required, marked the same way). On the left side make a list of the purposes and goals of the church. Begin with the most formal statements, such as a biblical covenant, liturgical creed, or the preamble of the church by-laws, if these are available and appropriate. Next list the formal goals that the official church boards may have accepted as targets for the current calendar year or for long-range programs. Finally, list your own informal statements of purpose. Many small churches will list only the informal purposes. These should include the satisfaction and services that the church provides for individuals, families and the larger community.

On the right side of the paper list the organizations and activities of the church. Begin with the most formal and official boards. Include all the Sunday school classes, fellowship groups, service clubs, and prayer circles. Note especially the larger and inclusive activities such as Sunday worship, family-night suppers, and annual events. Last, list the most informal groups, such as the sofa-sitters in the coffee hours, or the men who always have Sunday school class in the kitchen, or the families who share doughnuts and coffee every Sunday after worship.

Finally, match the two sides. Show the relationship between the goals and purposes on the left, and the church organizations and activities on the right. This can be indicated by using numbers for each of the goals and purposes on the left side, and letters for each group or activity on the right and then matching numbers with letters. Or it can be done by a carefree connection of lines drawn from each item on the left to the appropriate activity on the right.

Chapter Eight

The Ministry
of Goals and Purposes

Goals for the church are important mainly for the clarity that they provide. Goal statements make specific what purpose statements leave vague and general. Goals provide a clarity of purpose, a sense of progress, and a measurable standard for evaluation. They offer guidelines for the allocation of resources, and a standard of accountability for the organizational groups that make up the life of the church. Goal statements are especially helpful in the management of the church, and especially satisfying to those who feel the need for more clarity of general purposes.

Most small churches lack that kind of clarity in their statements of church goals. Yet they have deep commitments to the purposes of the church. In comparative studies,[1] smaller congregations distinguished themselves in their emphases upon a Christ-centered faith, the importance of Christian fellowship, and the urgency for the church to respond to people in need. Members of larger congregations emphasized programs and processes. For example, the larger congregations pointed to the importance of worship *per se,* to the need for an adequate education program, and to the urgency for the church to be clear on the issues.

Small churches have strong commitments. Some may have a statement of purpose in the liturgy. Many more find their purpose embedded in the things that they are doing, have been doing, and expect to continue doing: Sunday worship, Sunday school, pastoral care, response to personal crises, maintenance of building (care of cemetery), family events, prayer and study groups, women's organizations, the rhythm of official boards and informal groups. In a general way, they want to spread the gospel, preserve community standards, bind families together, be of use in the community and of service to the Lord. More than one has listed "training seminary students" as part of their purpose. Yet these are the things they are already doing.

One pastor complained, "I can't get them to talk about goals or examine what they are doing. But they don't stop, they just keep doing." One expert in industrial management process volunteered to help the representatives of a small congregation develop a statement of goals. When the retreat was over, he shook his head in disbelief and frustration. They had written a statement, but he doubted if it would ever be used. "They appear to be goal-less and drifting," he said, "and yet they are determined to survive, too stubborn to change, and quick to respond to a person in need. They may not have goals, but they surely have deep commitments to their church."

A look at the exercise "Church Groups, Goals, and Purposes" should be instructive. First, for individuals it will suggest those programs about which each person has the greatest interest—usually positive, but sometimes negative. The groups we support tend to be fulfilling more of our purposes, and those we doubt tend to be associated with marginal purposes, from our perspective. We discover that we need each other to be able to see the whole.

Second, official boards and committees (or task forces) tend to be associated with specific goals. Informal purposes seem more appropriately associated with informal groups. In general, the small church will have fewer goals as such, but several strong commitments to general purposes for groups in the congregation.

Third, goal statements are more important to groups with new members. Goal statements provide a second-hand substitute for newcomers who have not shared the experiences and crises well known to many older members of the congregation. Newcomers, including the pastor, often find goal statements very helpful.

Fourth, it should be clear that the caring cell can embrace a number of activities without losing touch with the members. Usually members are surprised at how much is really going on, especially in the areas of informal gatherings of people who mutually care for and support one another.

Commitment to purpose can sustain the small church over long periods of time. Goals are more appropriate if the church seeks to measure change and to feel a sense of accomplishment. Purposes serve maintenance functions, goals serve management functions. When compared to larger, more organized churches, the small church often has stated fewer goals. It is committed to people, not progress. Its purpose is appropriate to the kind of group that many small churches feel themselves to be. Technically, they can be said to be goal-less. But that should never be confused with the absence of determined purposefulness. To confuse the absence of goals with the absence of purpose is like suggesting that those who do not speak English do not know how to talk.

Members of small churches are often personally familiar with goal-setting procedures. Most have participated in some sort of goal setting in their places of employment, and many congregations have engaged in redevelopment programs based on clarity of purpose and measurable goals. Most denominational offices provide redevelopment materials, and many excellent books are available in bookstores and libraries. The approach and emphases are significantly different. For example, Robert C. Worley, in *A Gathering of Strangers* (Philadelphia: Westminster Press, 1976), concentrates on process and power; Donald P. Smith, in *Clergy in the Cross Fire* (Westminster Press, 1973), seeks to relieve the pressure of clergy role conflict; Lyle E. Schaller rolls with the changing times, from *The Local Church Looks to the Future* (Nashville: Abingdon, 1968) to *Survival Tactics in the Parish* (Abingdon, 1977).

Greater clarity of goals is particularly helpful (1) when the leadership is new, or new leadership is desirable (as in the entry process for pastors); (2) when the resources (usually money) are limited, and the board must make difficult decisions; (3) when a change is desirable in the informal character of the congregation; or (4) when growth is possible in the size of church membership.

Three areas of problems result from the implementation of goal setting in the small congregation, that need to be explored more fully. First, some members find difficulty in articulating the faith-ties that make the church worth attending. Second, the process elicits a new dimension of skills and relationships among the present leadership, and may produce another layer of church membership. Third, the process often precipitates aggressive and hostile emotions: the church may fight. I believe that these are natural conditions within the caring cell, but they are rarely considered in goal setting discussions that focus on larger congregations. To the rational planner, these responses may prove awkward or unexpected, even disastrous. Finally, I believe that the clarification of goals can have a positive use in the effective small congregation.

Printing the Unspeakable

"I tried to get the board to set down our goals," said the pastor, "but they just would not get specific." In another church a woman elder just sat there with her arms crossed. "It's really sacrilegious to put measurements on the power and love of God," she said. With a deep sadness, she continued, "I really don't feel right about this program." In another congregation the elder-teacher of a Sunday school class called the program "manipulation of feelings," and stated that the purposes of the church are "the same yesterday, today, and forever."

People who resist participation in the total process often fail to find the words for their disapproval. When they describe their reluctance, it usually falls somewhere among these six reasons.

(1) Some people do not like voting that divides the congregation. They do not mind voting when it affirms what they are doing together, or supports a report of some dimension in the life of the church. But they do not like to divide the house when forced to choose one of several people for one office, or to choose priorities among different church programs. They want to affirm the group, not divide the church family. One person wanted to know if we voted in making family decisions at home: "Do the kids vote with the parents, or do you wait until you know what is best to do as a family?" These members were more comfortable when given the choice among affirmatives, or when told "only the positive votes will count."

(2) Some people resist putting the purposes and goals of the church in anything other than biblical phrases or general statements. One person announced: "The real reasons I attend cannot be put into words, and I believe that is true for everyone. To write anything less than the truth is irrelevant." She was more comfortable when the leader distinguished between the "purposes of the church" (for which she attended) and the "goals" of particular church activities.

(3) Some people resisted systems, processes, procedures, committees, reports, resource allocation, and all management techniques. One urban ethnic member observed that it reminded him too much of the place where he worked, "with time clocks to punch in, and work sheets to fill out." He recommended that the church should live on "people time, which begins when we get here, and lasts as long as we can remember." He did not like what he called "creeping systemism." Only the informality of the group would bring him along.

(4) Some people objected to the way the goal-setting process emphasized the future. "Goal statements tend to emphasize what we will do, and neglect what we are doing," observed one pastor. A layman protested that "we

can't always plow up the present for the sake of the future, not every year." One old-timer objected that "goals are the 'game' of the pastor, and he doesn't even know us yet." These people were more at ease when they could see that the goals were an expression of the more permanent purposes of the church.

(5) Some people felt that the goal statements were too subjective and self-serving. Unless questions are carefully phrased, they suggested that we were submitting God to a referendum. "God is not up for election," said one vigorous young Christian. "The question is not, What do I want? or even, What do we all want? The question must be, What does God want of my life and of our lives together?" He suggested that even the purpose of the church must be subject to constant review in the light of the revealed Word.

(6) Last, there were people who felt that goal setting was a betrayal of the most basic relationship between people and pastor. In their view, the pastor who knows and loves his people will lead them right. He or she should not need to ask the congregation or the board to set the goals or the priorities on the church. The pastor should "know." As one grandmother explained: "I know what my family needs before they ask. God knows my needs even before I am conscious of that need. If you really knew and loved us, Pastor, you would not have to ask for a vote of the congregation. You should *know.*" The comment seems to originate from the same sort of person who would expect the pastor to visit her in the hospital even if nobody passed the word that she was there. In both cases she seems to be saying, "But you're my pastor, you should *know.*"

Goal setting can be helpful when (1) not everyone is expected to participate in the same way; (2) the identity from the past is unchallenged; (3) the present situation is seen as an opportunity, not a threat; (4) the decisions are not all made by vote; and (5) the responses are not all processed through organizational assignment. The relational style of many small congregations finds expression in government by "ad-hocracy": "He who will, let him respond." To change that style might treat people equally, but fail to touch them individually.

Levels of Leadership

Relational congregations have a "people first" style of making decisions. When the committees meet, the members spend much of the time getting caught up on the lives of other committee members, and members of their families, and members of their families' families. I remember a discussion that began with of the need to fix the church roof. It went like this: "Mr. Smith was the last person to get up on the roof and fix it." "You know his daughter moved to California, and left the old man alone." "I heard that his daughter is sick out there." "No, I believe that's her baby that's sick." "Baby's in the hospital out there, the way I heard it." The original item was the need to fix the roof. It provided a chance for several people to catch up on the Smith family. At many such meetings, most of the time is spent catching up on people. In the final five minutes, they decide about the program—as one pastor playfully says, "To do it again like we did it before—whatever 'it' was."

If personal relations provide the basic style in a congregation, goal setting will change it. Programs of congregational development bring order and intentionality into the official board meetings. The change is more than procedural. It changes the climate of the group and the satisfactions in its membership. Good management procedure brings out a different side of the existing leaders. It often brings out a different set of leaders. As one delighted pastor explained, "Goal setting brings out the best *in* our leaders, and the best *of* our leaders." Unfortunately, as we have seen, some members get lost in the shuffle.

In a general way, clarifying purpose and determining specific goals has a positive effect on the congregation. Many pastors have reported in their congregations the phenomena that have been studied by Litwin and Stringer in industrial settings: "Emphasizing group loyalty and group goals increased group identity and led to improved performance, less concern about personal regards, more mutual trust and less strain in interpersonal relations."[2] One pastor summarized, "It works."

It works better for some people than for others, and differently in each congregation. Group goals had a positive effect on some people and a neutral effect on others. Measuring achievements aroused some people to strong positive activity, and inhibited others. The combination of group goals and measurable achievements had an ambivalent effect upon the groups tested.[3] The observation is supported by the small-church studies of Theodore Erickson:

The response of most small churches . . . is genuinely ambivalent. There is a degree to which many small churches want to become more modern, improving their facilities, streamlining their decision-making capabilities, and increasing their membership. But there is a subjective component of small church viability that is often lost in our quest for measurable results. That component is the church's ability to embody values which are meaningful to its members, but not necessarily compatible with the corporate ethos. Small churches continually adjust in their own ways to new cultural environments, while at the same time contributing their values to society at large. Both the adjustments and the contributions come about through person-to-person relationships.[4]

Conflict over Goals

The ambivalence sometimes finds expression in conflict. Despite a variety of books, resources available in workshops, articles, and through consultants, the problem of conflict surfaces in every discussion of congregational development in the small church. "How can we deal with conflict," asks one pastor, "when it always seems to break out over very small matters?" Another pastor, well into the goal-setting process, complained, "Our congregation can handle the big issues, but we break up over the personal issues and petty arguments." It seems as if fighting is a natural way of life in the small church.

It is, according to the classic study of Lewis Coser. He says: "Conflict is a form of socialization. . . . Groups require disharmony as well as harmony, dissociation as well as association; conflicts within are by no means altogether disruptive factors."[5]

Small congregations prove particularly susceptible to social conflict. Members of a caring cell have relationships that are not personally threatened by the transitory fighting over petty concerns. The pastor who looks for an organizational solution does not appreciate the nature of the conflict. Thus, one rural pastor writes: "I keep hoping to find an organizational way to deal with conflict. We have a congregation of several large families, and the feuds are built in. Most of our conflict is petty and personal." That situation, is in Coser's view, "a stable relationship":

Stable relationships may be characterized by conflict in behavior. Closeness gives rise to frequent occasions for conflict, but if the participants feel that their relationships are tenuous, they will avoid conflict, fearing that it might endanger the continuance of the relation. When close relationships are characterized by frequent conflicts rather than by accumulation of hostile and ambivalent feelings, we may be justified, given that such conflicts are not likely to concern basic consensus, in taking these frequent conflicts as an index of the stability of the relationships.[6]

In other words, in a stable, healthy, trusting small congregation, they will not manage the conflict: they are free to fight. Further, Coser adds, in close proximity, the conflict may be more intense. Thus, they may not fight more often; but when they do, its a lulu. They are "free" to fight, because they are held by bonds that are deeper than reasons or issues.

Professional sensitivity to the appropriate pastoral response to conflict is a much too complex question to be considered adequately in this context. Donald E. Smith, in

Clergy in the Cross Fire, has gathered a wealth of relevant research materials. James Allen Sparks (*Potshots at the Preacher*) has processed many of the relevant questions in a most usable form. In general, some pastors provide a kind of objectivity that helps people separate reasoned arguments from prejudice, so that decisions may be reached rationally. Others have tried to sort out the causes of conflicts, which may reach back some years into the history of the relationships among the participants. They have tried to unravel the causes of conflict, much as a psychoanalyst seeks to sort out the causes of a personal character disorder. Other pastors have seen the goal-setting process fall victim to sharp differences in a congregation that long preceded the advent of any particular program: if one family was favorable, another family was already opposed! Some pastors have outlived the combatants. Others have simply withdrawn and looked for a call to another congregation.

Some small congregations have been helpful in humanizing young pastors beyond any education our seminaries can offer. Other congregations have a record of doing the opposite. They seem to chew up pastors, the old and the young alike. This second kind of congregation seems to be composed of families who have agreed to disagree violently but passively. Among themselves they have developed a social sickness we might call symbiotic animosity: they have learned to "enjoy" mutual enmity. In Coser's words, they need "hate objects," but not victory.[7] Among themselves they have evolved a relationship of cool cordiality that masks their deeper hostility. But woe to the program that gets tossed up between these families: they will destroy it. Woe to the unsuspecting pastor who tries to serve each family equally. The families need to hate each other, and the new pastor is grist for the mill. He or she will be chewed to pieces, although the cause of the conflict long preceded the pastor's arrival.

Coser's insights should not be lost: Stable small churches are free to fight. For the most part, the pastor does not cause the conflict. The pastor is simply not that important, at least in the first few years. The conflict "teams" were usually aligned long before the pastor arrived (there are always exceptional pastors who do precipitate fights—sometimes wherever they go). The pastor must be in touch with his or her personal feelings and be professionally prepared to seek a more durable settlement. Goal setting often precipitates the political realites that long preceded the advent of the process, or the pastor who raised it.

Goals and Purposes

Despite these liabilities and land mines, clarifying goals is one effective means to help a small congregation to mobilize its positive strength. As one pastor said in review of a year's work to sharpen the goals of the church: "For years the church had existed with each member assuming that he knew what the others felt. Now they had the opportunity to express themselves. They experienced a oneness in the Lord. Spiritually, it was a healthy experience."

Goal setting works. But in the small congregation the experience tends to be different in several significant ways.

First, the small church tends to be more conserving. Members of small churches want to see the relationship between church purposes and organizational goals. The more they treasure their experience in the past, the more they will want to see the connection between the proposed church goals and the proud history of the church. Goal setting is not just an organizational program; it must be a spiritual experience. The effects are noticeable first in the enthusiasm of congregational worship.

Second, older members in the congregation will play an affirming and surprising role. Unlike the age distribution in many larger congregations, in small churches the elderly are usually present and vocal. Often they have lived through many crises in the congregation and know the crosses that members still carry. They have seen pastors come and go, and remember "how we got to where we are." Older members offer two kinds of contributions to the process of congregational renewal. On the one hand, they honor the traditions but do not cling too closely to them. Younger church officers often want to "do things right." Often the elderly, given the opportunity to reflect, can have the large perspective. They know that we did not always do it this way. Further, in personal terms, the matriarchs and patriarchs can manage the first sergeants, when necessary. On the other hand, the elderly can provide a substitute source for the new ideas that other congregations may receive from a flow of new members. The elderly have imagination. They remember the images and models of the past when "we did it differently in Reverend Jones' time." In many small congregations the elderly offer the most liberated source for innovative alternatives to current programs. What's more, who is going to argue with their memories?

Third, the number of goals chosen in a small church is different, for goals serve opposite functions in the larger and the smaller churches. The large church will typically choose many major goals, smaller goals, objectives, and tasks. For the larger congregation, multiple goals provide the banners around which to rally the support of each of many different church groups. Multiple goals provide an appropriate basis for the several interest groups and tasks groups that make a larger church effective. Through many groups, it can absorb more people. The small church typically chooses fewer and different goals, for the opposite reason. In the small church the goals must serve to unify the congregation, not divide it. In other words, in the large church the whole congregation accepts the process and tolerates a diversity of goals. In a small congregation, the church accepts all of the goals, but only tolerates the process. What appears to be the same procedure serves opposite functions in larger and smaller congregations.

Fourth, small churches find more of their goals in what they are already doing. In larger congregations, goal setting often produces a whole harvest of new ideas. In the smaller church, the process often allows the congregation to hear themselves say what is important, so that they can concentrate their resources to do it better. The larger congregation needs quantity to keep going. The smaller church provides a different quality of care. Thus, the exercise at the beginning of this chapter often provides a flow of ideas: What is our purpose, formal and informal? What are we doing well and what could we be doing better? In the panorama of our possibilities, where is there place for innovation? When is it time to let something go? Church goals and purposes should judge the quality of church groups, and the real life of the groups should refine the accuracy of church goals. Matching should provide a simple way to view the strength of church life in an effective small church. Quality, not quantity, is the question.

Last, in the small church there is a much shorter loop between the perception of need and the capacity to respond. One pastor voices the experience of many: "When people see the human need, they have fantastic resources." Unfortunately, the inverse is also true: when people get discouraged, they become legalistic, demanding, and negative. Discouragement leads to despondency. The effective small church has found a way to use the short feedback loop to its advantage. They celebrate their victories. They feel a need, fill it, and then they celebrate. They celebrate because it feels good to be helpful. They come to think of themselves as helpful, sensitive to needs that can be filled. A wedding anniversary can be a cause for celebration, or a church dinner, the birth of a child, the end of school (or the return of school), the return of someone from sickness, a letter from a friend, or even the death of a life well-lived. In the small church, "if one member suffers, all suffer together; if one member is honored all rejoice together" (I Cor. 12:26).

The affirmation of purpose and clarity of goals should be an aid to the leadership of small congregations. It should support but never inhibit the spontaneous sharing of mundane victories and the quality of caring for people and parish, through which God liberates people from a sense of anonymous helplessness in the blur of the mass society.

For Further Reading

Coser, Lewis. *The Functions of Social Conflict.* New York: Free Press, 1956.

Schaller, Lyle E. *Parish Planning.* Nashville: Abingdon, 1971.

Smith, Donald P. *Clergy in the Cross Fire.* Philadelphia: Westminster Press, 1973.

Sparks, James Allen. *Potshots at the Preacher.* Nashville: Abingdon, 1977.

Worley, Robert C. *A Gathering of Strangers.* Philadelphia: Westminster Press, 1976.

Chapter Nine

Exercise: Church Fellowship Circles

Draw a circle to represent the largest number of people who participate actively in any one group that was shown on your church "map" (chapter 8). Let the size of the circle roughly represent the number of people who participate in that group. Label the form, and identify the number of *families* represented. You can use any group that appears on the map, including the official boards, committees, Bible study and prayer groups, and so on.

Draw another circle to represent two kinds of information. (1) Draw the size of the circle to represent the number of people involved in the group (as above). (2) Locate the circle in such a way that it overlaps the first circle in proportion to the number of *families* that are represented in both groups.

Thus the two groups might be represented in the following way:

Women's Organization 50 Family Units   Choir 9 Families

This would suggest that the Women's Organization had fifty active members, and the choir had nine active members. Members of six church families are active in both the Women's Organization and the choir (represented by the overlapping circles).

Proceed in this manner to draw all the groups that are included in the previous exercise (chapter 8) in such a way that they overlap in proportion to the number of *families* that are represented in the multiple groups. To make it easier: (1) Begin with the largest groups and those that overlap the most. (2) Do not limit yourself to circles but use any imaginable geometric form. (3) Do not expect to fit it together the first time, but draw several until you have one that appears accurate.

Chapter Nine

Turf Types of Churches

Church size, of course, is *not* the only factor in determining how a particular congregation will behave. The smaller congregations have much in common in the personal satisfactions of membership and the limitations of congregational activity. In their behavior, small congregations have much more in common with other small congregations than they have with larger churches in their community or in their denominations. But size is not the only or always the most important factor in determining the life-style of any particular congregation.

The determinative factors in any congregation are as complex as the members who attend. When asked what kind of a church a person attends, most people respond with objective information: either the denominational name or the geographic location. When asked why they attend most people respond with a subjective judgment of personal satisfaction or faith conviction. When asked why they chose a particular congregation, most people remember the invitation of a relative or friend. These elements of objective data, personal judgment, and social relationships become mixed to determine the life-style of a particular congregation. Like a person, the congregation has a character composed of its past experiences and personal expectations. With such a mixture, congregations never quite fit the categories that we offer to explain and predict their behavior.

Size has about the same influence on the character of a church that it has on the self-image of a person—it is more important for some than for others. Church size is most helpful when it is seen as one dimension among other forces that shape the church and affect its character. We will consider two other formative influences: one is ideological and the other sociological. In the context of character development, one cluster of influences is *inherited* faith and the other is *environmental* context. Each influence will provide a typology of churches through which the small congregation can discover kindred spirits, learn from those who are different, and raise its own sensitivity toward a higher quality of Christian caring. Church typologies should provide guidelines to aid church leaders and members discover a more helpful basis for comparisons among congregations.

Heredity and Environment

Each church inherits self-images and expectations that directly affect the life-style of the congregation. Denominational labels have historical meaning, and carry theological implications. Denominational ties provide polity, liturgy, trained clergy, membership requirements, an understanding of the sacraments, and a history of encounters between church and society. Even if the inheritance is rejected or denied, these historical expectations provide the context for whatever actions the local church may take. H. Richard Niebuhr, in *Social Sources of Denominationalism,*[1] has helped many of us to appreciate our heritage. His descriptions of social conditions in which the churches have ministered offer insight into separate denominations and perspective upon the larger contributions of Christianity in America.

Based on the biblical and historical experience of the church, a second kind of inherited self-image is found in the theological typologies of the church. I mention only two sources: the monumental study by H. Richard Niebuhr, *Christ and Culture,*[2] said to be a theological reflection on his earlier work mentioned above; and the recent, provocative study by Avery Dulles, *Models of the Church.*[3] These and similar books provide the pastor and concerned layperson with theological resources to separate and compare churches that differ in their perception of the world and in their practice of the faith. They are important primarily because they articulate and reflect the theological typologies shared by many clergy in America.

However, environmental influences seem to many analysts to be even more important in determining, or at least in predicting, the behavior of many congregations. Most books on church types reflect the dominant influence of demographic factors on the life-style of the congregation. Books are legion on the town-and-country church, the urban church, the Old First church, the new suburban church, and so on.[4] This literature assumes that the kind of community dominates the type of Christian witness that will be effective. Further, they point out that when the community changes, the church has difficulties in continuing to reach the new population with an appealing message. Other books try to be helpful to congregations caught in communities in transition.[5]

The most helpful church typologies attempt to combine both the inherited characteristics and the environmental influences. In *Parish Planning*, Lyle Schaller offers such a list:

Today, even an elementary listing of the categories of church types would include the metropolitan church . . . , the downtown "First Church" . . . , the neighborhood church in the central city or older suburb . . . , the nationality or language congregation, the black church . . . , the "gathered congregation" that is trying to perpetuate yesterday, the specialized urban congregation, such as the university church, the intentional nongeographical urban parish, the "Memorial" church dominated for decades by one person or one family, the new suburban mission, the church in a racially changing community, the long-established congregation on the rural-urban fringe, a fifteen- or twenty-year-old suburban congregation, the "First Church" in the county seat town, the small, open-country congregation, the church in the small trading center, and the church in the dying crossroads village.[6]

When inheritance and environment are combined, the number of church types stimulates the imagination but overloads the memory. Too many types make the analysis unmanageable.

Douglas Walrath, in his excellent article, "Types of Small Congregations and Their Implications for Planning," helps to untangle the problem with his suggestion for "a three dimensional classification system . . . (1) social context, (2) social position and (3) church organization."[7] Walrath describes twelve types of social context, each with demographic characteristics, patterns of population change, and characteristic church. The twelve locales are designated: mid-town, inner city, inner urban neighborhood, outer urban neighborhood, city suburb, metropolitan suburb, fringe suburb, fringe village, fringe settlement, independent city, rural village, and rural settlement. The logical progression and supporting data provide an orderly framework for considering the importance of each environment on the nature of particular churches.

But environment alone is inadequate. In his brief discussion on social position, Walrath suggests that congregations can be distinguished by the attitudes toward their location. "Social position may be defined as the 'posture' or position of influence that a congregation has in relation to the community or neighborhood to which it relates."[8] The suggestion parallels a second approach to typology offered by Schaller: "It is also possible to cut the cake in another direction and to define such categories as the growing congregation, the family church, the dying church, the subsidized church, the church in mission, and the churches which . . . minister to certain distinctive life styles in society."[9] In the context of the small church, I believe that the most fruitful approach to the problem of combining ideology and environment lies in the comparison among congregations based on the attitude of the members toward the place where the church is located. The combination of faith and place produces "turf types" of congregations. Without violating the most fundamental uniqueness that is the character of each congregation, church types based on turf commitments may provide a basis for helpful comparative studies among small churches.

Turf Types: Regional and Local

A layperson who served on the council of a larger parish once described turf types of churches that participated in the council. He said: "We all gather in our churches, but we gather differently: One church is a gathering *in* the community, and another is the gathering *of* the whole community. One of the churches gathers *from* the community, and others gather *from several* communities. The last church is a gathering of an *ethnic 'clan'* who live throughout the whole area. They meet in an open country church, and everyone is welcome who can find it, and speaks 'dutch' [deutsch]."

These different ways that churches gather provide the basis for a typology of small congregations. For our purpose, the attitudes of people toward the turf of the church can be separated into two broad categories: Some people attend a church that draws its membership from throughout the region. They share a faith based on their common cultural heritage, their denominational commitments or their personal Christian experience. They are not confined to a specific geography or "parish boundaries," but have a concern to attract all kindred spirits from throughout the area. They are regional churches.

Other people choose a church that has a more specific and identifiable geographic base. They gather in a chuch that is "of" the community, or at least it is "in" the community. Cultural and denominational interests are secondary to sharing the faith with people with whom they share the community. Their sense of church turf is local and defined by specific boundaries. They may not be able to share their particular faith with everyone in that turf, but they share with them a concern for everything that happens in that space. It is their common parish.

Regional churches and parish churches reflect a basic difference in the way people gather into congregations. But within each of these two broad categories, several distinctions must be made. We shall discuss three kinds of *regional* appeals. One is the *Old First Church* of the denomination, the first, clearest, and proper expression of that faith group in the area. A second regional church is represented in the *ethnic congregation,* which is open to anyone who can find it and speaks the language. The third regional appeal is found in the *high commitments* of gathered congregations who base their faith primarily on personal conviction and private experience. These three kinds of congregations all draw members from regional areas. All three may show the same total membership, but they have vastly different styles of Christian life and witness. They "gather differently."

By comparison, we will consider three attitudes toward the turf that may be found in *local* parish churches. The basic attitude is that they belong to the land, and the land belongs to them. The first type of parish is *stable.* Unfortunately, there are not many stable communities. The neighborhood church is affected by two additional attitudes toward their parish turf. One is positive, which anticipates *growth* in the population of "our sort of people." The Protestant church has demonstrated a remarkable aptitude for helping our new families in growing communities assimilate into the fabric of the neighborhood. We have recorded this as church growth. The other attitude toward change in the church turf is negative. It anticipates a *decline* in the population of our people, hence a decrease in the number of prospective members of the congregation. Thus neighborhood churches view their parish as stable, growing, or declining. The way they perceive their relationship to the land will shape the self-image and program options for the congregation.

Regional: Old First or Grace Church or Holy Trinity

Old First Church does things properly, with style. It may have a tall steeple, a high pulpit, a pipe organ, a robed choir, and a printed (not mimeographed) bulletin—even if only twenty-five people attend. Old First is the voice and witness of the denomination. The congregation can appeal to people from throughout the region, regardless of their ethnic, racial, or economic background. Members tend toward educational similarities and often have old family ties. These churches are the denominational cathedrals that gather those who appreciate "the best."

Old First does not "solicit for members," but she does absorb new people through a process of adoption. Prospective members are often attracted by the quality of special programs that Old First provides. Budget in Old First often comes from endowment. Yet membership will contribute to maintain a proud ministry, when asked at a congregational-community dinner, or through mail solicitation. The line between church concerns and community concerns is never precise, and community groups often meet in the church buildings. Although it is clear that many of the community leaders belong to Old First, it is not always clear who does not belong. One pastor of Old First noted that the "work of the church is easily shared with many people who are not officially members, but they care." He carefully designated that community people have willingly accepted "nonofficial, short-term tasks of ministry."

Regional: The Ethnic Family Church

The ethnic church is a cultural family at prayer. When they gather, time stands still. They have a wide building, a variety of musical instruments, several strong singers (or several choirs), a charismatic leader, and no printed program at all. The choreography and momentum of their worship is every bit as old and fixed as the worship in Old First Church, but very different. They may have a turf association with a particular building where they worship. Or they may share a memory of a place that is long ago in their lives—a town in the south, a valley in Puerto Rico, a village in the old country. The roots to their culture are often stronger than denominational connections. One pastor wonders, "Since the church has moved so often, I fear that our people are more loyal to culture or rather to an ethnic God, one that is present only in their particular language and their form of worship."

Ethnic churches receive new members by adoption into the larger family. The same pastor envied the importance of the church in the lives of the members, old and new: "They belong to the church and become part of its life, and it becomes a part of them." New members often discover the church through annual events and family crises. In ethnic churches there are many "annual members" and no sustained effort to distinguish between church membership and family caring. One pastor of an ethnic (black) congregation reported that his church achieved positive results when he began to pastor without a membership roll. "Evangelism," he said, "begins with pastoral care. We came alive when we made unofficial members of everyone who shared in the ministry of the church. Our caring was done mostly through church families anyway."

The absence of clear membership lists makes pledging difficult, but it extends the family to include a much larger constituency. In addition, about 25 percent of the income for this congregation was raised in popular annual events, which also attracted a much larger constituency. Ethnic congregations sometimes perceive themselves as oppressed minorities and appeal to denominational sources for additional income. They have a well-earned reputation for survival in the midst of adversity.

Regional: The High-Commitment Church

High commitment congregations are a mountain of energy determined to move the world by faith. They often articulate clearly the meaning of membership and the mission of the church. Members make substantial commitments of time and resources to witness to their faith and achieve their stated goals. The intensity of their commitments provides a sharp contrast and a viable alternative to more traditional churches. They are gathered from the world and for the world.

Membership in a high-commitment congregation is a personal decision involving self-denial and discipline. Prospective members learn about the work of the church through reputation. High commitment congregations place a premium on the articulation of their faith. They often publish their own materials or purchase them from independent sources. Old First Church seeks a kind of denominational purity, the ethnic congregation expresses a cultural purity, and the high-commitment church expects a personal religious purity. Because of the clarity of their faith and the energy of their activities, high-commitment churches often attract disproportionate attention from the media, casting a negative shadow on other kinds of small churches.

In fund raising, they are clearly unique: only tithes, gifts, and offerings—no bazaars or cookie sales. They often focus their attention on particular spiritual and social problems in the community, for which they organize a program that they staff by their own volunteer members. High commitment congregations often locate in communities where their help is needed, but they deny that the place of worship has any significance for them. The funds of these congregations, which are not sustained by either turf or tradition, last as long as the commitments of the members. Their witness is awesome while it lasts.[10]

Local: The Stable Parish Church

The stable parish provides the model of turf identification: the church is a gathering in the community and of the community. The church and community share a concern for the families and individuals who live there, and for the resources that make a community viable. The stable community church reflects the interdependence of families and the soil, which have cared for each other for several generations. For better or for worse, few such idyllic communities exist in the economy of our land.

We are a mobile nation, and no community is exempt from change. Family farms and decentralized industry have allowed some rural families to stay on their land and support the neighboring economy. Some metropolitan communities have remained relatively stable if anchored in common ethnic ties and parochial, middle-class institutions. There appears to be relatively little mobility at the extreme ends of the economy: the landed gentry and the persistently poor. The appearance of stability in other communities often masks the quiet, short hops that families make up the rungs of their dream of economic success. Statistically the populations appear the same. Only the people have moved; about half of them move every five years.

Typically the church in the stable community has a widely scattered and aging membership. The church must work hard to keep up with the changes, stay even in membership, and reach the people who might respond to their invitation. The church community is not easily defined. It is a geographic area, but not everyone will respond. It is a community of faith, but never limited to those who have made a confession. In rural areas, the parish may pulsate with the influx of seasonal residents. In urban areas, the weekday contacts among members may become less frequent and more difficult. The church community is increasingly difficult to define and to reach with the gospel.

Effective churches in relatively stable communities usually become identified with the community groups that use their buildings. One urban pastor describes a strategy of using neighborhood buildings for church projects and encouraging the neighborhood groups to use the church building. He called it "getting the church into the community, and the community into the church." Lyle E. Schaller in his excellent book for parish development, *Hey, That's Our Church!,*[11] suggests that the keys to effective ministry lie in the self-identity of the congregation and a careful analysis of the potential members. Even the church in the stable community cannot simply wait to be found by the community.

Local: The Growing Neighborhood Church

When the community is expanding, or when the population is turning over rapidly, the effective church provides services that newcomers need and appreciate. On the one hand, they assimilate families rapidly into the friendship fabric of the community. On the other hand, they provide the necessary connections with family doctors, automobile repair shops, hardware stores for hard-to-find items, and dentists for the inevitable check-up. The church can help the transplanted family take root in the community. With minimum effort and organization, churches in growing communities have thrived

Some churches in these communities have decided not to increase beyond a fixed membership of about one hundred fifty people. They have accepted many of the community values of trained leadership, efficient planning, easily digested materials, measurable results, and continual evaluation. But they have made a conscious decision not to grow beyond the number of people who can keep in touch with one another, who can know one another personally. They replace members who move out, but they have not grown beyond the single caring cell.

In many ways they resemble the high-commitment congregation. They are intentional about their activities and concentrate on specific community concerns, such as day-care facilities, youth programs, and mental health. Funds are pledged annually, often by telephone canvass of the congregation. They have a clear sense of their mission.

149

As one pastor says, "We need a mission to stay alive." He goes on: "We know that we are not the most important group in the community, but we are important to each other. If we stopped serving others, we would smother to death." Not mission, but financial commitments usually precipitate a felt need for more members.

Local: The Declining Neighborhood Church

Why Can't They Be Like Us?[12] is the challenging title of Andrew Greeley's hard-hitting study of white ethnic consciousness in mobile America. The recognition that "they" and "us" are different creates the most perplexing problem that confronts the witness of small churches. Communities are often increasing in total population; but when the newcomers are not responsive to "our" sort of churches, the neighborhood is seen to be "declining" by the members of the church. Because of cultural differences in religious expression, the church is caught in an apparently impossible choice: It will not succeed in attracting people simply by trying a little harder. It might reach new people if it changed its program and approach, but the changes might alienate the members who remain. To keep their scattered members, they need excellent transportation and an usually appealing program. To survive the cultural transition, they need substantial investment of human energy and financial resources. Even then, a happy ending is not assured.

Churches in "declining" neighborhoods feel that their turf has been invaded. Too often they have been driven indoors, with an edifice complex about their building, and a series of storm appeals for money. Further, the congregation often carries grief for lost members whom the most recent pastor does not know and has never met. Even if they are successful in reaching a few of the new population who have moved into the community, they often discover that the people who have responded to them are the most dissimilar to the other recent arrivals. The first of the newcomers to join are often the least able to reach the others, and the least interested in trying.

Churches that perceive their communities as declining are typically located in two distinctly different situations: one is in the older residential areas of the city, and the other is on the rural-metropolitan fringe. Both see themselves as islands of faithful witness in a sea of human need and religious indifference. Although the populations may be growing, both congregations perceive their communities as declining because "our sort of people" are not moving in.

Churches on the rural-metropolitan fringe have discovered great differences in program and pace between families who have lived in a comunity all their lives, and those who are relatively recent arrivals. To reach the new residents, fringe churches must accelerate the pace of the program.

Small churches in the city are often faced with the opposite situation. Both church and community have usually aged together, offering opportunities for service primarily among an elderly, more casual population. To provide needed care, many urban congregations have slowed down their pace and expanded their hours. One city pastor described the turning point: "We concentrated on the elderly, widows and widowers. We started where we hurt the worst, and these 'people issues' touched other people. When they got turned on, the response has been overwhelming."

Churches in changing communities generally discover the need for a vision greater than their own, and for resources beyond membership. Vision and resources will be discussed in our final chapter, after we have considered the program implications of fellowship circles.

Fellowship Circles and Membership Doors

In the following illustration, I have suggested two basic approaches that are often used in response to the exercise. One drawing (A) is characterized by a variety of overlapping circles, several of which drift off into space, without a clearly defined line between the fellowship groups, the church membership, and other people in the community. Another (B) is characterized by a solid border for the membership, fewer overlapping circles, and a unique figure in the center (as a square or a star) to designate the official board.

In general, the loose fellowship circles that drift into the community reflect the self-perception of congregations that feel comfortable in their geographic or cultural communities. These include the ethnic congregations, the stable community churches, and young congregations in new communities. By contrast, some congregations seek to organize the fellowship groups according to their functions in the program of the church. These include the Old First Church (which is organized by the book), the high-commitment church (which has a purpose for every group), the church in the declining community (which seeks refuge in order), and the church in the rapidly changing community (for whom the structure provides a continuity while the people are changing). One style is not superior to another. Each style is appropriate to cope with different conditions.

Comparisons between these turf types of churches should be helpful to relieve unwarranted criticism and generate new directions for appropriate styles of program in different situations. Some danger signals can be noted in the column on the right of figure 2.

Sometimes the groups are found to overlap too much (C), making additional membership virtually impossible. The membership capacity of a congregation is based upon three items that should be clear from your drawing and your knowledge of the congregation: the number of groups, the space in those groups that does not overlap with other groups, and the commitment of those groups to make a contribution to the life of the church and the health of the community. That is, the drawing will show the capacity for

EXAMPLES OF FELLOWSHIP CIRCLE EXERCISE

HEALTHY SMALL CHURCH DIAGRAMS	DANGER SIGNAL DIAGRAMS

(A) Most often found in
    ethnic congregations
stable community
    churches
new, growing
    community churches

(C) too much overlap
    inadequate entry space

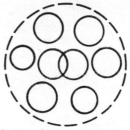

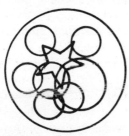

(D) inadequate informal
    contact
    loss of trusted
      communication

(B) Most often found in
    denominational Old
    First
high-commitment
    church
church in declining
    community
church in rapidly
    changing population

(E) loss of organizational
    personnel
    gaps in skill or
      decision making

growth, but only commitment will provide the energy for growth.

The typical growing congregation shows fellowship circles spread out at some distance from the center of the drawing. Church leaders make the point that the growing congregation has groups in various stages of constant formation and dissolution. Further, these groups are visually at some distance from the watchful eye of the official board, since they are forming and disbanding upon the initiative of leadership from within and are only loosely connected with the authority structures of the church.

A second dangerous condition exists when the fellowship circles within a congregation have drifted apart (D) and show no family overlap at all. These conditions are typical of merged congregations and congregations on the rural-metropolitan fringe. Church groups may be reached through official communications from the pastor or church leadership. However, misunderstanding and conflict are highly likely without a more trusted source of information from within the group. Some overlapping of family participation in small church groups greatly facilitates the level of trusted information.

A third dangerous condition (E) exists when the church has been so highly structured that the work of each group is dependent upon a clearly authorized and trained occupant for each program position. The small, caring-cell church has a place for everyone in the fabric of the group, but anyone may be expected to do what is to be done. The more highly structured congregations may have defined the work of the church so functionally that only qualified people can fill in these gaps. For the small church in the changing community, such careful organization may prove disastrous.

In addition, the drawings also suggest which groups in the congregation have accumulated decision-making power. As the circles are drawn (and redrawn to accurately represent the overlap of church families), the fellowship group that migrates to the center of the cell has accumulated the most informal power in making policy for the church. Through the group in the center, the official actions of the church are disseminated, and from that group the concerns of the church are articulated. This power may be in the official board, but it is equally likely to be in the Sunday school, the women's association, or the choir. Church leadership would do well to take stock of those who sit in the center as they listen to the congregation and develop purposes, goals, and programs for the church.

Further, in small-church workshops it has become obvious that some congregations can be strong without being active, since turf types differ in their styles of participation. When we consider levels of attendance at various functions, we receive the following estimates from pastors and church leaders:

	Average Sunday attendance	Fellowship groups participation	Annual/ Special events
Old First Church	30%	50%	80% + guests
Ethnic church	50%	30%	120% + friends
High-commitment church	70%	80%	90%
Stable parish	35%	50%	60% + guests
Growing-community church	40% + visitors	60% + visitors	80% + visitors
Declining-community church	25%	30%	40%

Also turf type churches take different attitudes toward relationships with other congregations: Regional congregations will cooperate with other churches, but they will not easily engage in long-term yoked parishes or ecumenical federations. Parish churches, with greater clarity of boundaries, are more easily joined in ways of mutual economic benefit.

The particular turf types can be compared in the countless different ways they witness to their separate understanding of the Christian faith. We have noted a few similarities and differences concerning fund raising, membership recruitment and participation, and community service. These congregations can also be compared in worship and liturgy; in leadership styles and recruitment; in their annual and special events; and in their sense of place, pace, history, and architecture. The comparisons are endless, instructive, and fun. I am continually impressed in workshops with the way that the laity can compare these types with greater clarity than can the ordained clergy. Perhaps the clergy have been called to serve the universal church, but the laity have chosen freely the particular church that best expresses who they are.

Church types are important because they help identify appropriate programs, and relieve the anxiety created by inappropriate expectations. But even more, the recognition of our own identity helps us discover how much we need one another. No one type, no one theology, no one denomination can do it alone. In confessing our uniqueness, we discover how much we need others to find the fullness of the Body of Christ.

For Further Reading

Dulles, Avery. *Models of the Church.* Garden City, N. Y.: Doubleday, 1974.

Niebuhr, H. Richard. *The Social Sources of Denominationalism.* New York: Meridian, 1957.

Schaller, Lyle E. *Hey, That's Our Church!* Nashville: Abingdon, 1975.

Walrath, Douglas. "Types of Small Congregations and Their Implications for Planning," in *Small Churches Are Beautiful,* ed. Jackson W. Carroll. New York: Harper, 1977.

Chapter Ten

Exercise: Tensions Between
Denominations
and
Small Churches

Draw a rough representation of the animal that best expresses your feelings about the behavior of the denomination.

Draw a rough representation of the animal that best expresses your feelings about the behavior of your congregation or small churches in general.

Draw these two animals in a posture of trying to relate to each other.

In light of the above cartoon, please list:

How does the small church see the denominational relationship, and how does the denomination see the small church? What frustrates each the most? What has each to offer to the other?

In other words, how can these two critters live together helpfully?

Chapter Ten

Are Denominations "Viable"?

Often small congregations are challenged to prove that they are "viable" as a requirement for receiving denominational support. The question is put most frequently to those churches seeking financial aid. If the small church is, as we have suggested, a primary group of caring Christians, then the question might better be put in the opposite direction: Are denominations "viable" as partners in the ministry of small churches?

Sharp tensions should be obvious between denominational organizations and the leadership of small churches. One reason is that they are very different kinds of human groups: denominations are secondary organizations (the sociologist Max Weber called the church hierarchy "classic bureaucracy"). Small congregations are single, caring cells—classic examples of strong, primary group relationships. These two different kinds of groups see each other very differently, often with a touch of condescension toward the other.

Thus, small church leaders are likely to see themselves as fortunate to be part of a "real Christian fellowship," where people are more important than program, where growth is measured in decades and generations, where God is surely present. Sometimes they see the denominational structure as bureaucratic machinery that squeezes people for money, expects the impossible overnight, and spends most of its energy on petty arguments. Conversely, leaders of the denomination are apt to view themselves as stewards of the Lord's resources, applying facts and reasons to difficult problems, and using mature management to develop strategies, allocate resources, and generate careful evaluation. For them, the small church is sometimes archaic, clannish, emotional, petty in its arguments, and much too affectionate to be efficient agents of mission. Even the compliments reflect the tension—for example, the consultant who said that "the small churches always have the best cooks, but they never seem to eat on time, or finish eating."

The tension between the primary and the secondary group is much older than the current misunderstanding between denominational offices and small churches. We should recognize its ancient roots in human behavior and "enjoy" its day-to-day expression without getting personally disturbed. If that were the only cause of disagreement we could simply rejoice that each group is well scripted and provides what the other needs most. Unfortunately, there is more.

Mutual Distrust

There is a second, more disturbing level of basic disagreement about the problems the small church faces. Consider this dialogue: The denominational leader might complain that the small church always does things "the same old way," and yet "they want a full-time pastor, at our expense." The small-church leader feels that the "denominational hierarchy is always changing something, including the minimum compensation for clergy, and yet we have to pay the bills for the church *and* the pastor." The small church may recommend "the obvious course, that we have a part-time preacher for a hundred dollars a week." The denomination suggests that hiring a part-time minister is shortsighted investment. "One hundred dollars a week is one hundred dollars an hour," and that equals the death of the church. They recommend that the congregation raise additional funds, with the help of the denominational office. The church responds that "We are doing all we can." So it goes . . .

Beneath this dialogue are currents of distrust and hostility. Some denominational leaders feel that small churches may not be worth the investment of time and resources. "Small churches take up most of my time," said one church executive, "which would be all right if I had anything to show for my efforts. They are inefficient and out of step, even with each other." Another church official resented the "double jeopardy" of trying to be helpful: "I am criticized in the denominational committees for having so many churches that need aid, and criticized in the small churches for trying to help them become self–sufficient. I am caught in the middle and get a lot of grief from everyone."

Leaders and pastors of small congregations also show their distrust of and hostility toward the hierarchy. They often express feelings that denominational staff are "headhunters," looking for a reason to cut the funding that some congregations need. Sometimes they express deep personal doubts about the sensitivity of church executives who "never like the pastoral ministry" or "never really wanted to be close to people anyway" or "always wanted to be Mr. Big with a buck." Among my most difficult moments have been the confidential conversations with local church leaders on the one hand, and denominational leadership on the other, each raising questions about the others' motives and intentions, resources and abilities, skill and sensitivity, honesty and personal integrity.

Small-church pastors and denominational officers often find it convenient to distrust and dislike each other. In many situations, each provides a convenient scapegoat for the other. Coser suggests that the "evocation of an outer enemy or the invention of such an enemy strengthens social cohesion that is threatened from within."[1] I do not know how widespread such feelings are, but I know they are "ecumenical," explosive, and, in my mind, unnecessary.

Small-church pastors and denominational executives have more in common than they have to divide them. They are both ministers (administrators) caught in the middle between the same irreconcilable expectations. One is called by the local congregation, the other by the denomination. But both are key figures in the continued ministry of small churches. They could make life much easier for each other.

A first step toward the resolution of the denomination/small-church problems lies in the simple admission that each will serve the Lord better when both agree to disagree honestly, openly, and without personal innuendo, in a spirit of Christian love. They have more to offer when they share their differences in perspective and resources. Neither alone can deal with the problems that confront small churches and concern the whole church of Jesus Christ.

Now, what were those animal drawings for the small church and the denomination? A squirrel and an elephant? A porcupine and a giraffe, or a 'possum and a bear (or vice versa)? How about a couple of badgers who can't make it alone but aren't sure how to live together?

Denominational Perspectives

Denominations can serve congregations in two general ways: by a wider perspective on their ministry, and by specific resources for their mission. Perspective is one dimension that the small, local church lacks. They may know much more about their own situation, but they rarely know how that situation compares with others. The denomination can help the local church see its ministry in the context of the whole church.

Information on conditions (issues, resources, pending changes) in the community provides the local church with its context for ministry. By involving members of small churches in the processes of the denomination, the judicatory creates arenas for dialogue. Each can learn from the other. In areas of our study, the small congregations actually had more members *per capita* serving on committees, commissions, and agencies of the judicatory than did the larger congregations. These small-church members often gained perspective on local church problems by serving with the judicatory committee. But their insights were lost to the local congregation, because the congregation did not know how to use their experience. For some members, it was consoling just to learn that other congregations have problems "just like ours."

Pastors particularly need to be drawn into the informal sharing of the denominational and ecumenical clergy groups. Pastors who feel down about a particular congregation need to share their story with others who have stories of their own. Pastors who confront a continually discouraging situation seek supportive friends outside the particular setting in which they serve. Several judicatories have found that supporting the pastor's spouse was even more important in the low spots of their ministry.

A more formal perspective is provided by sharing models of specific congregations and studies of alternative programs for changing situations. The farmer-elder who says "we grow more corn and fewer people every year" must know that he is not alone in facing that condition. The congregation that is perpetuating a service no longer needed should be shown how others have reshaped their ministry and redirected their energy. Leaders of the church on the metropolitan fringe, where new families are being frozen out by old-timers need to talk with pastors who have lived through it elsewhere. Local congregations need the kind of vision and perspective that denominational structures are able to provide.

"We don't need more programs," said an elderly officer of a local congregation. "What we need from this denomination is contacts with people who have been there, and examples of what they did; and, above all, we need wisdom to help us make decisions." He called wisdom the "missing rung on the ladder" between the denomination and the local congregation. Wisdom is perspective refined by experience.

Denominational Resources

Perspective is invaluable as one resource for the small church. But something more tangible is also expected.

Denominations have physical resources that are available to all who share the denominational family. But resources are not free. Denominational resources carry a price tag of money and of independence, and small churches have difficulty letting go of either. Denominational resources can be grouped into four areas: ordained clergy, lay training and program materials, staff and consultant service, and financial support.

Ordained clergy are the most important denominational resource. The Lord calls the pastor, the congregation feels the call, and, in some cases, the bishop (or his representative) hands it out. But the denomination has a general responsibility for the preparation of the clergy, for the quality of clergy leadership, and for the continuing education of those who have been called. The presence of ordained clergy in good standing signifies a kind of legitimacy to a congregation that may otherwise feel threatened.

The importance of ordained clergy is reflected in the percentage of available resources that the small church will spend. Sometimes more than 80 percent of the budget will be devoted to the pastor's compensation. Even more, the small church of fewer than one hundred members will give money far out of proportion to its size if it has the remote hope of securing a pastor of its own. It is this commitment that gives rise to the general belief that small churches give more. They do, if they can reach the necessary income to have a resident, ordained clergy—the recognizable symbol of denominational acceptance. Without that incentive, their giving is below average.

Denominational resources also include the training and enrichment of the lay leadership of the congregation. State and regional meetings, weekend retreats, summer conferences, Bible camps, special conventions and assemblies all contribute to the preparation and growth of laity as leaders in the local congregation. Such programs allow church membership to share their perceptions of the church, their pride in a Christian history, and their vision of the future for the Christian witness. Often overlooked by most members of small churches, these meetings provide a resource of understanding and commitment that brings the denomination together and can strengthen commitment to the local congregation.

Denominational staff and special consultants are also available to local congregations. Most denominations have attempted to locate staff personnel where they are immediately accessible to the needs and interests of local congregations. Since the demand for their services is not usually initiated by invitations to small congregations, denominational staff have more often invested time in denominational projects and in working with those congregations where they feel they would be welcome. Denominational personnel universally say they would respond gladly to more invitations to work with small churches.

Finally, denominational resources include money in cash grants and bank credits. Available funds create an ambivalent relationship between the denomination and the congregation. When the church needs money, the price is local independence. Often the local church feels that the denomination is a cross between Sugar Daddy and Big Brother—they are "sometimes ready, and always watching."

As in a marriage, the distribution of money precipitates the most difficult decisions. In an effort to be fair and equitable in the distribution of available funds, denominations have tried to determine objective bases for funding local churches and other projects. In order to evaluate their investment, they have tried to define "the viable church."

The Viable Church

"Viable," a term borrowed from the life sciences, carries a range of connotations, from "barely able to survive" to being "full of life" and "ultimately capable of sustained growth." The term is associated with congregations for the purpose of measuring and comparing congregations to determine which should receive support from very limited benevolence funds. Measures of viability usually seek to evaluate three dimensions of the situation: the *need* for that particular witness, the *cost* to the local church and to the denomination, and the *will or determination* criteria, and yet they provide the rationale for later decisions. Most measures of the viability of a church focus on the will or determination of the congregation to follow through, and usually use one of the following approaches in assessing the *viable commitment* of the congregation.

One approach uses an objective, statistical measurement. This procedure asks not for total figures, but for percentages. For example, it will ask the percent of membership present at an average Sunday worship, the percent of Sundays when the laity assist in worship leadership, the percent of cumulative income of church families that is received in the church budget, the percent of pledging families, and the percent of leadership attendance in denominational meetings. (Incidentally, in one denomination the "viable church" has been set at 50 percent worship attendance, 25 percent lay leadership of worship, 5 percent of family income to the church, 100 percent pledging families, 100 percent attendance at denominational meetings—all considerably above the national averages.) Other objective criteria include the use of the denominational hymnbook, denominational Sunday school literature, denominational fund-raising materials, denominational procedures for program planning and evaluation, and the development of a ten-year plan for the congregation. The criteria are objective, and the standards far exceed denominational norms. Surprisingly, many small church leaders find this approach relatively comfortable. They do not measure up, of course. But once they get by that hurdle, as one church officer said, "In percentage participation, we can always hold our own."

A second approach to measuring viability seeks only to determine the regularity of the congregational process. It asks the church to certify the regularity of worship, of Sunday school, of church board meetings, of reports to the church boards, of the administering of the sacraments, of attendance at denominational meetings, of elections for officers. Such a measure is often welcome because it trusts that appropriate programs will result from "regular process." A variation is to ask if the congregation has a "system" for pastoral care, a "process" for planning, a "program" for evangelism, a "plan" for stewardship. This approach avoids the sticky problems of trying to make comparisons of appropriateness and effectiveness among situations that are basically different and among personnel who have very different gifts.

A third approach to viability is based on the mission of the congregation. Commitment is measured on the basis of the accuracy, integrity, or impelling description of the request for funding. Admittedly, the reports accompanying these requests are more exciting to read, and may have a side effect of generating additional resources in the authors (as they convince themselves) and in the readers (as the reports are circulated throughout the judicatory). Some requests emphasize the need, others the resources already available, others the special skills and interests of both pastor and membership. In general, the denominational staff seems more involved in developing these requests and more enthusiastic about their result. The trust level between denominational staff and local personnel seems higher, but usually the congregation was informally selected by denominational staff before the written request was initiated. The mission request may be more stimulating than a statistical report but there is no evidence that it is more accurate in predicting the future of the church.

Each style of measurement examines a different dimension of the small church. The first looks at the hard core of church membership and compares it with others. The second looks at the pace and endurance of the membership to see if it will last for the long haul. The third asks for enthusiasm for a particular task at a particular time with a particular leadership. As these elements change, these criteria may be less helpful. All three approaches to measure viability should be considered when funds are allocated for long-term ministry through small congregations.

After great effort has been invested to be fair, equitable, and sensitive to congregational request, the results are rather disappointing: denominations still cannot determine which congregations should be supported and which can be allowed to "pass away." The congregations often have the feeling of receiving too much attention—as one member said, "like radishes that are pulled up every few days to see how we are growing."

The Problems of Money

Most small churches pay their own way. With meager resources and maximum effort, congregations retain their financial independence. In fact, the largest number and the heartiest of small churches are in those denominations where funds are simply not available. Edward Hassinger found in his study of small rural churches that the introduction of denominational procedures, including financial support, seemed to reduce the resolve of the congregation to retain its independence.[2]

Different denominational patterns reflect slightly different purposes in the distribution of funds. For example, the Methodists offer incentive for the funds to "roll over" more quickly, while the Baptists are willing to leave low-interest loans to the congregations, providing this investment in the title will encourage the local congregation to participate in denominational programs. Conversely, local churches often find incentive in burning the mortgage and going off the "dole." Several pastors reported that the church income increased when they held out the promise that we are almost on our own.

When financial support is made available for small congregations, it comes, as one church treasurer pointed out, "to the largest item in our annual budget, the pastor." Throughout all mainline Protestant churches, the subsidy is provided for the pastor's salary. Even when it is designated "aid to churches," the supplementary funding ceases when the pastor moves to another calling. In the face of this almost universal practice, I wish to lodge a personal protest. Funding for the pastor usually involves measuring the viability of the congregation. The practice is degrading, and the results are doubtful.[3] Rather, the congregation should be expected to finance the cost of its own ministry. This should include the expenses of a building and program materials, of benevolence and that part of the pastor's time which is needed by that congregation. The remaining proportion of the pastor's professional time should be contracted in other forms of ministry.

Two sources have been widely used to broaden the base from which the small-church pastor can receive the full professional income: tentmaking ministries and clustering churches.

Tentmaking Ministries

"No less than 22% of pastors, more than one of every five, engages in secular employment in addition to their parish ministry."[4] These startling statistics, based on the 1974 Clergy Support Study of mainline denominations in the National Council of Churches, were assembled by Robert Bonn and his associates. It marked a 50 percent increase in the tentmaking clergy in the past decade and demonstrated a basic shift in the attitudes of those who served in bivocational ministries.

The Pauline model of the independent, self-sufficient ministry (Acts 18:3, 20:34) was the inspiration for the worker-priest movements in the earlier part of the twentieth century in Europe and later in the United States. These movements sought to reach the alienated industrial worker. Tentmaking was more than an alternate means of financial support. It provided entrée to the laborer's world.

Tentmaking came to symbolize an ideological breach with the establishment bourgeois church and the management values that sustained it.

Quietly, a dramatic change has taken place among those who feel themselves called to be tentmakers. They do not leave the church in order to find their ministry. Rather they seek additional responsibilities to fulfill of themselves and extend their calling. Further, they do not feel alienated from the organizational dimension of the church. The contemporary tentmakers tend to be management-oriented and institutionally employed as professional people. They have spent more years in higher education and hold more advanced degrees than clergy who have a single calling.[5] On the whole, they are a remarkably gifted group of pastors who felt underemployed with a single vocation.

Three brief comments seem appropriate for those who are interested in further exploration of this option. First, it is far more pervasive than any denominational statistics suggest. Even within the same denomination, identical circumstances might be recorded as "temporary," "auxiliary," "supply," "vacant," or might even escape any special designation at all Congregations may act unilaterally to make an arrangement with a student, hire a retired cleric, or borrow a pastor from another denomination without reporting to or receiving a response from denominational authorities. In his epilogue to *Case Histories of Tentmakers,* James Lowery accurately reports, "Mainline denominations simply could not operate in many jurisdictions without the constant support of and use of tentmaking clergy."[6]

Second, tentmaking relationships are difficult to initiate, and almost impossible to transfer from one pastor to the successor. An extensive and sensitive study, Clergy Occupational Development and Employment (CODE), has been developed in Rochester, New York, with the support of seven judicatories of four denominations.[7] The program was designed to train pastors for tentmaking opportunities, develop suitable job opportunities, and assist congregations in the transition. Two results are clear: Far more tentmakers already existed than were known to denominational leaders, and far fewer additional people were interested in the opportunity. In three years, one person went through the program. It appears that judicatories might encourage those who find themselves called to be tentmakers, but not attempt to design an ecclesiastical channel for developing tentmaker clergy.

Third, tentmaker ministries may prove most significant in providing a model for dual assignment contracts within the denominational structures. The pastor of a small congregation can combine a contract with a parish for part of the time, along with a contract for some other phase of church or judicatory program. A number of such dual contracts have proved very successful when pastors are also responsible for managing summer camps, developing youth ministries, consulting in Christian education with other congregations, developing ministries of care, or organizing support systems for pastors and spouses. In these dual contracts within the church structure, the pastor has many of the same satisfactions as the tentmaker: he or she feels that professional skills are more fully utilized, and the congregation no longer feels that they are on "ecclesiastical welfare."

Clustering Churches

The theological imperative, as Marvin Judy calls it, for the cooperative parish of small churches "lies at the point where people of God in different congregations within a given geographic area find a means of ministry to all the people and all the needs of the people within the area."[8] Clearly this is the gospel, as Judy carries us step by step through the process of being sensitive to the community and aware of different alternatives for structuring the larger parish. The book is more helpful as an advocate for clustering congregations to bring the Christian witness in word and deed.

Enthusiasm for gathering churches into meaningful ministry has been echoed by others.[9] One pastor noted that "we have seen great things happen when needs have been identified, objectives formulated, and programs launched to meet our goals. It was wonderful."

Fortunately one such cluster of churches has been studied extensively over a three-year period.[10] Although the study includes congregations of only one denomination (Reformed Church in America) located in the rural fringe of one upstate community (Albany, New York), the careful data-gathering and painstaking analysis offer unique insights into the strengths and weaknesses of clustering churches. In using this material I am not concerned with the kinds of structures through which churches may cluster, or the complications of ecumenical efforts. Rather, I emphasize the effects of clustering upon the perceptions and satisfactions of clergy and members in this particular setting.

The situation was typically rural, i.e., changing and troubled. The synod was faced with "an increasing number of small congregations which appear to be more and more unable to function independently." The five congregations were sufficiently different, yet "appeared to have histories typical of congregations located in suburban fringe places . . . did not seem to be attracting new people very well . . . having difficulty with church school, with program for young people, and in holding the quality of pastoral leadership." The project examined the quality of leadership and program, the development of pastoral leadership, and the role of the denomination in supporting the clustering of churches.

In one sense, the project was a resounding success: the programs expanded in quality and variety. More people participated in cluster programs, and in separate church events. New people attended, and older members became more active. The pooling of resources gave confidence for more adventuresome efforts, and the ventures proved successful. People came. Pastors felt the momentum pick up. Above all, the pastors enjoyed the new depth of relationship that developed from working together, sharing their concerns, and contributing their own unique gifts of ministry as needed in the common effort. They especially appreciated the organization of a common office in the community around which they worked. Professionally and personally, they became very attached to one another and to the cluster of churches.

The church membership had a very different view of the three-year experience in clustering congregations. Their reactions should not surprise anyone who has attempted to cluster churches. Their feelings also provide a kind of summary for the small-church dynamics that we have considered in this book.

First, the most frequent comment concerned size: "Cluster programs were too big. . . . Size was overwhelming."[11] People had a sense of being lost in the crowd. In commenting on the reaction of one congregation, the analyst summarizes: "The cluster, which tended to break up this close knit community, as people spread their efforts and their activities across a larger group, was a counterproductive experience to people in this highly active, close knit, small congregation." The caring cell of the church family had been broken.

Second, there was the "issue of pace . . . the increase in activity which eventually became a burden." Everything was right to do, but "there was so much to do, and it all had to be done so quickly."

Third, the members were uncomfortable about the cluster office. The pastor was less local and less available than he had been when his office was in the manse. The actual distance was not the issue. Turf was at stake, and they had lost him to a neutral turf.

Fourth, the members felt that something was broken in the "exclusive relationship of pastor and congregation." One typical comment related to seeing the pastor in the cluster office: "The tight band between minister and congregation has been broken. Now it's like going to see a businessman."

Fifth, the pastors experienced some of the same grief in the lost intimacy with the congregation and the difficulty of working closely with colleagues. "None of us anticipated how difficult it would be. . . . Working in a team is a difficult and sometimes threatening experience."

Sixth, the church boards voted against continuing the project. They had not seen evidence that it *materially* (financially) helped or *spiritually* enriched the churches of their responsibility. In Judy's theological imperative for clustering, nothing was said about local church councils that vote *no!*

Last, more people were participating, but they were not assimilated into the congregations. The report summarizes the dilemma: "New residents and non-members . . . do not have the same traditional ties of family and community roots which encourage participation by longstanding members. Therefore, the cluster, with its high quality programming, is an important attracting point for new members and an important ingredient in bringing the churches toward a fruitful future. . . . On the other hand, preserving a close knit, supportive congregational life in individual churches is equally important." Not either/or, but both/and.

The partnership of congregations may be a way to a fruitful future, as in the cluster described above. But in at least two urban situations the same process has been used to take the sting out of the final years of ministry for aging congregations. The pairing of a dying congregation with a stronger church gives each a new dimension of caring for the other, and together they have a Christian ministry that will outlive both. The same procedure that can give new life to one church can provide an appreciative departure for those whose ministry has reached its conclusion in the other. As the psalmist said, "Their works live after them." Literally, the stronger churches absorbed the history and the membership of the older, not by merger but by voluntary partnership. Eventually the silent history was transferred, the old building was liberated, and new worshipers are creating their own events worth remembering.

Local Independence

"They act so independent, and yet they have so many 'needs.' I never know how to relate to small churches," complained the denominational program developer in the farm belt. His ambivalence reflects the confusion of an outsider looking at the single cell of caring Christians. In the most thorough study of rural churches available, Hassinger maintains that independence of small churches is not an accident:

The characteristics of local congregations' program may insulate them from the influences of the larger society. Programs tend to be turned inward emphasizing the worship service. . . . The ubiquitous Sunday school is another evidence of self-maintaining, characteristic of the church programs. Sunday schools can be a completely laymen's activity. . . . Resistance to complex organizations was also apparent in the lack of official boards in many churches and the irregularity of their meetings in still more.[12]

By a conservative theology, concentration on caring for members, low overhead on the building cost, and minimum expenses for professional clergy, small churches have maintained their autonomy. Hassinger continues:

As denominations seek to influence local congregations to conform to their models of program and organization, some congregations may opt and have the ability to disassociate themselves from the denomination. . . . In reformulating our conception . . . we finally regard the congregations as primary groups.

What Hassinger has seen in rural congregations could serve as a summary for the attitudes and commitments of most small churches elsewhere. They have found a way of ordering the world and caring for members, for conserving experience and coping with change. Hassinger proclaims with prophetic insight:

It is hazardous to predict the future of the [small] church but its tenacity in a changing society suggests that another survey in a decade would find the bulk of the congregations operating at the same stand and in about the same level of activity. They will continue to be essentially fellowship groups engaged in internal activities and a frustration for denominational executives.[13]

Hope of something better springs from experiences such as those recorded by the Small Church Project sponsored by the United Church Board for Homeland Ministries. After working with fifty congregations for three years, the staff summarized the problems they found and the prospects for change:

We need to recognize that current staff functions are failing to produce acceptable relationships with local pastors and local congregations. . . . Most congregations are not being strengthened and . . . current staff styles are not aiding them. . . . Churches do not necessarily want professionals, they want friends with professional skills. . . . They want competent people who feel their needs, understand their dreams and share with them in seeking ways to realize their potential. . . . It is not so much what we do that frees congregations but who we are in relation to them. The key to change in local congregations is the intentional development of loving relationships among staff, pastors, congregations and their leaders.[14]

A Summary
Small-Church Perspectives

I have tried to describe the way that small churches have restored a basic dimension to the fullness of biblical theology. Small churches have reclaimed the importance of times, events, and history. Small churches have memorialized the significance of people, land, and particular places.

Small churches have retained the good vibes, rhythms, seasons, and experiences worth remembering.

In a big world, the small church has remained intimate. In a fast world, the small church has been steady. In an expensive world, the small church has remained plain. In a complex world, the small church has remained simple. In a rational world, the small church has kept feelings. In a mobile world, the small church has been an anchor. In an anonymous world, the small church calls us by name—by nickname! As a result, small churches have survived where others have failed.

Small-Church Challenges

Small churches offer such an attractive image of Christian relationships that larger congregations often claim to duplicate the experience. They say, "We are a collection of small churches; come and see." Usually the groups they create are temporary and task oriented. They provide what Alan Toffer has called instant intimacy. In what they seek to do, larger congregations have been successful, judging by membership statistics.

Ultimately, larger churches are not like small churches. Even "a collection of small churches" never offers the same feeling as belonging to a small congregation, where everyone is known by name as part of the social fabric. Larger churches should be commended for choosing such high ideals. They can do many things exceedingly well. But larger churches can never duplicate the single cell of a small Christian congregation.

Sometimes even the small church cannot live up to its own expectations. The small church is a caring cell, or at least it can be. "Caring" challenges the church to be genuinely inclusive. Do the pastors and the people really see one another in the choreography of worship, or do they focus on only a few selected people? Are new members really adopted, or do they remain step children with only their Father in heaven and no room to call their own? Is the pastor as lover left waiting in the anteroom of important decisions? If order provides the bones of continuity in the social body, then what would you say about a church where only order remains? Christian love can be measured, I believe, by the inclusive quality of the congregation's caring.

Small churches have a theological genius for conservation. They find their identities in past events, their roots in significant places, and their strength in the pulse of regular events. The quality of their Christian character can be measured by the strength of their positive identity as people who have found a place in God, to be used for the healing of others in need.

The challenge of coping is to remain effective, not simply to survive. Every congregation should be strong enough to affirm its identity, spiritually and financially. Yet every church should also be sensitive to the fact that it needs the larger, denominational and ecumenical church to be its partners in reaching others. Coping challenges us to partnership with the community where we are, the larger church that embraces the world, and the power of God, which transcends us all.

Small Church Resources

Small churches have a unique quality of Christian love. They are not always nice; yet they never let go. In a community of high mobility, small churches suffer. As the economy slows down, small churches offer an alternative way of life.

In the early 1970s, when the national economy experienced a recession, many national companies were forced to delay moving their young executives every three years as expected. This had three interesting effects in one newly constructed suburb that provided the residence for many young management families. First, the moving-van companies were off about 30 percent in their anticipated business. Second, the social counselors and pastors of the community experienced a marked increase in the number of people who had crises in their marriages, apparently related to crises in career advancement. Third, the nurseries who sold plants and bushes noticed a dramatic increase in the sale of trees. For the first time in that new suburb, people began to believe that they would live there long enough to enjoy the shade of their own trees.

Small churches can't thrive where people keep moving. But there is a place for small churches in a world where people plant their own trees.

For Further Reading

Judy, Marvin T. *The Parish Development Process.* Nashville: Abingdon, 1973.

Lowery, James L., Jr. *Peers, Tents and Owls.* New York: Morehouse-Barlow, 1973.

———. *Case Histories of Tentmakers.* New York: Morehouse-Barlow, 1976.

Madsen, Paul O. *Small Churches—Vital, Valid and Victorious.* Valley Forge, Pa.: Judson Press, 1975.

Waltz, Alan K. "Organization Structures for Small Membership Congregations," in *Small Churches Are Beautiful,* ed. Jackson W. Carroll. New York: Harper, 1977.

NOTES

1. Perspective on the Small Church

1. James L. Lowery, Jr., *Peers, Tents and Owls* (New York: Morehouse-Barlow, 1973), p. 89.

2. *Ibid.*

3. Lyle E. Schaller, "Looking at the Small Church: A Frame of Reference," *Christian Ministry,* July, 1977, p. 6. "The most widely used criteria to define the 'small' church:

(1) number of members

(2) worship attendance

(3) a comparison with past days when the congregation was much larger

(4) the image projected by the pastor's definition of comparative church size

(5) the size of the building

(6) the size of the budget

(7) a full workload for the minister

(8) an individual's previous experiences in other congregations

(9) the quality of caring relationships among the members

(10) the size, number, and variety of fellowship circles or primary face-to-face groups which together constitute that congregation."

4. Lyle E. Schaller, "Twenty Questions for Self-Evaluation in the Small and Middle Sized Church," *Church Management,* April, 1977, p. 18.

5. Schaller, "Looking at the Small Church," July, 1977, p. 6-7.

6. Using figures from United Methodist, United Presbyterian, Episcopal, General Conference Mennonite, and Evangelical Covenant Churches.

7. Large churches are not confined to suburban growth. For example, Mennonite, Lutheran, and Baptist congregations often reach distinctive size in rural areas, while many African Methodist Episcopal and National Baptist churches have grown proportionately in urban areas.

8. *Membership Trends in the United Presbyterian Church in the USA* (General Assembly Mission Council, United Presbyterian Church, USA, 1976), p. 81.

2. The Caring Cell

1. Charles H. Cooley uses this familiar quotation to introduce the concept of the "primary group" in his earlier *Social Organizations* (New York: Free Press, 1956), p. 23. Later the quotation is preceded by a notation that seems appropriate to a discussion of the small church: "The chief characteristics of a primary group are:
   A. Face-to-face association;
   B. The unspecialized character of that association;
   C. Relative permanence;
   D. The small number of persons involved;
   E. The relative intimacy among the participants." Charles H. Cooley, Robert C. Angell, and Lowell J. Carr, *Introductory Sociology* (New York: Scribner's, 1933), p. 55.

Cooley's concept of the primary group is particularly appropriate because of his concern for formation and confirmation of individual values in the context of a variety of intimate group settings: the family foremost, but also the play group, the gang, the school and the neighborhood. It is more limited than the "community" (*Gemeinschaft*) defined by Ferdinand Tönnies, and more value oriented than the "folk society" discussed by Robert Redfield, although both authors have greatly influenced this discussion. For additional reading on uses of primary group, see: Michael Olmsted, *The Small Group* (New York: Random House, 1959); Edward A. Shils, "The Study of the Primary Group," in *The Policy Sciences,* ed. Daniel Lerner and Harold D. Lasswell (Stanford: Stanford University Press, 1951), pp. 44-69; John C. McKinney, "Introduction," in *Community and Society,* by Ferdinand Tönnies, ed. and trans. Charles P. Loomis (East Lansing: Michigan State University Press, 1957), pp. 1-29; Avery Dulles, *Models of the Church* (Garden City, N. Y.: Doubleday, 1974), chap. 3; "The Church as Mystical Communion."

2. Theodore H. Erickson, "New Expectations," in *Small Churches Are Beautiful,* ed. Jackson W. Carroll (New York: Harper, 1977), chap. 10.

3. Cooley, *Social Organizations,* p. 24.

4. Erickson, "New Expectations," pp. 162-63.

5. Lewis Coser, *The Functions of Social Conflict* (New York: Free Press, 1956), pp. 95, 104 ff.

6. Olmsted, *The Small Group*, p. 63.

7. Robert Ardrey, *The Territorial Imperative* (New York: Dell, 1966), pp. 217-18.

8. Julius Fast, *Body Language* (New York: Evans, 1970), chap. 4, "When Space Is Invaded."

9. In the use of pews and the development of meaningful space, entirely different perspectives are provided by John H. Westerhoff, III, and Gwen Kennedy Neville, *Generation to Generation* (Philadelphia: Pilgrim Press, 1974), chaps. 5 ff.; and Thomas Oden, *The Intensive Group Experience* (Philadelphia: Westminster Press, 1972), chaps. 1 and 5.

10. Peter L. Berger, *A Rumor of Angels* (Garden City, N. Y.: Doubleday, 1969), p. 66.

11. *Ibid.*, p. 67.

12. *Ibid.*, p. 69.

13. Olmsted, *The Small Group*, p. 23. "Most primary groups are small . . . but not all small groups are primary."

14. Milton Meyeroff, *On Caring* (New York: Harper, 1971), pp. 2, 54-55.

3. Growth by Adoption

1. Kurt Lewin, *Field Theory in Social Science*, ed. Dorwin Cartwright (New York: Harper, 1951). For the theoretical basis for this chapter, I am especially indebted to Kurt Lewin's Field Theory in general, and his concept of gatekeepers in particular.

2. Arthur Vidich and Joseph Bensman, *Small Town in Mass Society* (Princeton: Princeton University Press, 1968), pp. 251-52.

3. Schaller, "Looking at the Small Church," *Christian Ministry*, July, 1977, p. 7. "Chemists use the term 'supersaturated' to describe a solution in which the concentration of the solid dissolved in that liquid is abnormally high. . . . [The small church] is a 'super-saturated' group with more members than normal face-to-face primary groups can hold."

4. C. Peter Wagner, *Your Church Can Grow* (Glendale: Regal, 1976), pp. 85, 92.

5. *Ibid.*, chap. 7.

6. Allan W. Wicker, "Assimilation of New Members in a Large and a Small Church," *Journal of Applied Psychology*, Vol. 55, No. 3, pp. 151-56. See also Wicker *et al.*, "Size of Church Membership

and Member's Support of Church Behavior Settings," *Journal of Personality and Social Psychology*, Vol. 13, 1969, pp. 278-88; Wicker, "Organization Size and Behavior Sitting Capacity as Determinants of Member Participation," *Behavioral Science*, Vol. 17, 1972, pp. 499-513; and Wicker *et al.*, "Effects of a Merger on a Small and Large Organizaton on Members' Behaviors and Experiences," *Journal of Applied Psychology*, Vol. 59, No. 1, pp. 24-30.

7. Theodore H. Erickson, "Identity in the United Church (mimeograph 'by the Board of Homeland Ministries, United Church of Christ, no date) has made the helpful and historical distinction between covenant and contract. A contract consists of specific articles of agreement, is written, and is legally enforceable. A covenant is an agreement to "walk together."

8. Lyle E. Schaller, *Hey, That's Our Church!* (Nashville: Abingdon, 1975), pp. 34-38, 93-96, *passim*.

4. Pastor/People Tensions

1. See further discussion of conflict in chap. 8.

2. Jackson W. Carroll and James C. Fenhagen, "The Ordained Clergy in Small Congregations," in *Small Churches Are Beautiful*, ed. Carroll (New York: Harper, 1977), chap. 5.

3. Vidich and Bensman, *Small Town in Mass Society* (Princeton: Princeton University Press, 1968), p. 233, 234.

4. Carroll and Fenhagen, "The Ordained Clergy in Small Congregations," p. 78.

5. Herbert C. Gravely, Jr., and Spencer R. Quick, *The Use of Organizational Development Consultations/Small Mission Congregations*, Project Test Pattern, June 11, 1973, published by Alban Institute, Mount St. Alban, Washington, D.C., p. 3.

6. *Ibid.*

7. Alan K. Waltz, "Congregational Structure for the Small Congregation," in *Small Churches Are Beautiful*, p. 153.

8. James Melvin Palmer, Sr., "An Analysis of Selected Factors Related to the Elaboration of Congregational Structure" (Unpublished thesis, Mississippi State University, 1969), p. 130.

9. Julius Fast, *Body Language* (New York: Evans, 1970), chap. 4. "When space is invaded . . ."

10. Donald P. Smith, *Clergy in the Cross Fire* (Philadelphia: Westminster Press, 1973), chap. 4, "Internalized Role Conflicts."

11. Vidich and Bensman, *Small Town in Mass Society*, pp. 229,

235, 266 ff. Also see "The Churches of Midwest, Kansas, and Yoredale, Yorkshire," in *Change in the Small Community,* ed. William J. Gore and Leroy C. Hodapp (New York: Friendship Press, 1967).

12. See William A. Gamson, *Power and Discontent* (Homewood, Ill.: Dorsey, 1968), on the question of overt power and covert influence.

13. Henri J. M. Nouwen, *Creative Ministry* (Garden City, N. Y.: Doubleday, 1971).

14. Some pastors' spouses enjoy the stories. Sometimes they even provide an additional source to enrich the stock and contribute to the growing image of the pastor as a "real character." For a further discussion of the pastor's spouse under pressure, see James Sparks, *Potshots at the Preacher* (Nashville: Abingdon, 1977), chap. 7, "Criticism and the Minister's Wife."

15. Carroll and Fenhagen, "The Ordained Clergy in Small Congregations," pp. 75 ff.

5. Memory and Ministry

1. Michael Olmsted, *The Small Group* (New York: Random House), pp. 53 ff.

2. Sometimes the nickname serves to reinforce the position that a person holds in the group, such as the use of the man's last name rather than his first. What would be formality for some is intimacy for others.

3. See the discussion the "Viable Church" in chap. 10.

4. Gwen Kennedy Neville, "The Sacred Community—Kin and Congregation in the Transmission of Culture," *Generation to Generation* (Philadelphia: Pilgrim Press, 1974), pp. 51-71.

5. W. Lloyd Warner, *The Family of God* (New Haven: Yale University Press, 1961).

6. G. Ernest Wright and Reginald H. Fuller, *The Book of the Acts of God* (Garden City, N. Y.: Doubleday, 1957).

7. G. Ernest Wright, *The God Who Acts* (Chicago: Alec R. Allenson, 1952), p. 18-24, 33-58, *passim.*

8. Wright and Fuller, *The Book of the Acts of God,* p. 25.

9. Thomas Oden, *The Intensive Group Experience* (Philadelphia: Westminster Press, 1972), p. 100.

10. Wright, *The God Who Acts,* p. 13.

11. Lyle E. Schaller, *Survival Tactics in the Parish* (Nashville: Abingdon, 1977), p. 137.

12. See Max Thurian, *The Eucharistic Memorial* (Richmond: John Knox Press, 1961), especially Vol. 1, chap. 2, and Vol. 2, chap. 1.

13. Wright and Fuller, *The Book of the Acts of God,* p. 224.

14. Auburn Studies in Education, *No Idle Pastime—Guidelines for Projects in Local Church History* (Philadelphia: The Presbyterian Historical Society, 1974), Publication No. 4.

6. Places of Ministry

1. Walter Brueggemann, *The Land* (Philadelphia: Fortress Press, 1977), p. 5.

2. Paul Tournier, *A Place for You* (New York: Harper, 1968), pp. 45-46.

3. For example, the different emphases of Walter Brueggemann, in *The Land,* and W.. D. Davis, *The Gospel and the Land* (Los Angeles: University of California Press, 1974).

4. Brueggemann, *The Land,* p.

5. Tournier, *A Place for You,* p. 79.

6. A fuller discussion of the importance of place, accompanied by an excellent bibliography, can be found in Lyle E. Schaller, "Human Ethology: The Most Neglected Factor in Church Planning," in *Review of Religious Research,* Vol. 17, No. 1.

7. Max Thurian, *The Eucharistic Memorial* (Richmond: John Knox Press, 1961). The summary is found in Vol. I, chap. 2, "The Memorial as a Liturgical Form," pp. 20-26.

7. Events Worth Remembering

1. W. Lloyd Warner, *The Family of God* (New Haven: Yale University Press, 1961), p. 383.

2. John H. Westerhoff III and Gwen Kennedy Neville, *Generation to Generation* (Philadelphia: Pilgrim Press, 1974), pp. 96-97.

3. *Ibid.,* p. 97. See also fig. 1, p. 99, "Institutional Cycles in American Society."

4. Warner, *The Family of God,* p. 357.

5. Westerhoff and Neville, *Generation to Generation,* pp. 83.

6. *Ibid.,* p. 98.

7. Warner, *The Family of God,* p. 363.

8. Westerhoff and Neville, *Generation to Generation,* pp. 62 ff.

9. Gail Sheehy, *Passages—Predictable Crises of Adult Life* (New York: Dutton, 1974, 1976). Gail Sheehy raises all the same

questions of rites of passage that the community, the caring cell, has anticipated with rites of passage. The startling differences are: Sheehy has no elderly (and no one "goes home to Mama"), no blue-collar families, and no church or other support communities. Her models are mobile, middle-class, management Americans. Conversely, if we were a society of caring cells, there would be no market for her book. Compare her thinking with the work of Gwen Neville, and especially Westerhoff and Neville, "Life Cycle and Ceremonial Events," *Generation to Generation*, fig. 2, pp. 104-5.

10. Warner, *The Family of God*, p. 75.

11. Westerhoff and Neville, *Generation to Generation*, p. 68.

12. *Ibid.*, p. 44.

13. Mircea Eliade, *The Sacred and the Profane* (New York: Harper, 1961), p. 63.

14. I am especially indebted to Mr. Burton Symth, of the Support Agency, UPCUSA, for help in describing the Step-Up Program in particular, and for stewardship information in general.

8. The Ministry of Goals and Purposes

1. Douglas W. Johnson and George W. Cornell, *Punctured Preconceptions* (New York: Friendship Press, 1972), chap. 3, "Parish Expectations."

2. George H. Litwin and Robert A. Stringer, Jr., *Motivation and Organizational Climate* (Boston: Harvard University Press, 1968), p. 60.

3. *Ibid.* See especially chap. 4, "Dimensions of Organizational Climate," and chap. 6, "Leadership Style and Climate."

4. Theodore H. Erickson, "From Process to Covenant," *Christian Ministry*, July, 1977, p. 14.

5. Lewis Coser, *The Functions of Social Conflict* (New York: Free Press, 1956), p. 31.

6. *Ibid.*, p. 85.

7. *Ibid.* See especially chap. 3, Proposition 11, "The Search for Enemies," pp. 104-10.

9. Turf Types of Churches

1. H. Richard Niebuhr, *The Social Sources of Denominationalism* (New York: Meridian, 1957).

2. H. Richard Niebuhr, *Christ and Culture* (New York: Harper, 1956).

3. Avery Dulles, *Models of the Church* (Garden City, N. Y.: Doubleday, 1974).

4. Books on church-types by location include:
Ezra Earl Jones and Robert L. Wilson, *What's Ahead for Old First Church?* (New York: Harper, 1974); Craig Ellison, ed., *The Urban Mission* (Grand Rapids: Eerdmans, 1974); Gaylord B. Noyce, *Survival and Mission for the City Church* (Philadelphia: Westminster Press, 1975); Gaylord B. Noyce, *The Responsible Suburban Church* (Westminster Press, 1968); Gibson Winter, *The Suburban Captivity of the Churches* (Garden City, N. Y.: Doubleday, 1961); Robert Lee, ed., *The Church and the Exploding Metropolis* (Richmond: John Knox Press, 1965); Robert Lee, *Cities and Churches* (Westminster Press, 1962); Robert E. Moore and Duane L. Day, *Urban Church Breakthrough* (New York: Harper, 1966); Walter Kloetzlie, *The City Church* (Philadelphia: Muhlenberg, 1961); Edgar R. Trexler, *Creative Congregations* (Nashville: Abingdon, 1972); Rockwell C. Smith, *Rural Ministry and the Changing Community* (Nashville: Abingdon, 1971); David M. Byers and Bernard Quinn, *Readings for Town and Country Church Workers* (Washington: Glenmary Research Center, 1974).

5. Books concerning ministry in changing communities include:
Robert L. Wilson and James H. Davis, *The Church in the Radically Changing Community* (Nashville: Abingdon, 1966); Elisa L. DesPortes, *Congregations in Change* (New York: Seabury, 1973); Loren B. Mead, *New Hope for Congregations* (New York: Seabury, 1972); Grace Ann Goodman, *Rocking the Ark* (New York: United Presbyterian Church, USA, 1968).

6. Lyle E. Schaller, *Parish Planning* (Nashville: Abingdon, 1971), pp. 167-68.

7. Douglas Walrath, "Types of Small Congregations and Their Implications for Planning," in *Small Churches Are Beautiful,* ed. Jackson W. Carroll (New York: Harper, 1977), p. 34.

8. *Ibid.,* p. 42.

9. Schaller, *Parish Planning,* p. 168.

10. Dan Baumann has written an excellent study of several substantial high-commitment churches: *All Originality Makes a Dull Church* (Santa Anna: Vision House, 1976).

11. Lyle E. Schaller, *Hey, That's Our Church!* (Nashville: Abingdon, 1975).

12. Andrew M. Greeley, *"Why Can't They Be Like Us?"* (New York: Dutton, 1975).

10. Are Denominations "Viable"?

1. Lewis Coser, *The Functions of Social Conflict* (New York: Free Press, 1956), p. 110.

2. Edward W. Hassinger, Jr., Kenneth Benson, James H. Dorsett, and John S. Holik, *A Comparison of Rural Churches and Ministers in Missouri Over a 15-Year Period* (Columbia, Mo.: Research Bulletin 999—College of Agriculture, November, 1973), p. 23. See also "Resources: Income and Facilities," pp. 14-17.

3. See the discussion in Paul Madsen, *The Small Church—Vital, Valid and Victorious* (Valley Forge: Judson Press, 1975), pp. 116 ff.

4. Robert L. Bonn, "Moonlighting Clergy," *Christian Ministry*, September, 1975, p. 110.

5. *Ibid.* See also Robert L. Bonn and Ruth T. Doyle, "Secularly Employed Clergymen: A Study in Occupational Role Recomposition," *Journal for the Scientific Study of Religion*, September, 1974.

6. James L. Lowery, Jr., *Case Histories of Tentmakers* (New York: Morehouse-Barlow, 1976).

7. The participating judicatories included: American Baptist—Monroe Association and Niagara Frontier; United Church of Christ—Genesee Valley; Episcopal Diocese of Rochester; United Presbyterian Church—Presbytery of Genesee Valley; United Presbyterian Church—Presbytery of Geneva; United Presbyterian Church—Presbytery of Western New York.

8. Marvin T. Judy, *The Parish Development Process* (Nashville: Abingdon, 1973), p. 29.

9. Those interested in clustering in particular, and small church–judicatory relationships in general, might find additional help in the following materials:

Clusters: Guidelines for the Development of Local Church Clusters (Published jointly by the Board of National Missions, UPCUSA, and the Board for Homeland Ministries, UCC, May, 1970).

Strengthening the Small Church for Its Mission. A Report of the Task Force on Ministry to the Small Church to the 113th General Assembly, Presbyterian Church, U.S.

Special Report: The Small Church. Published by Synod of the Lakes and Prairies, Office of Communication, 8012 Cedar Avenue South, Bloomington, Minn. 55420.

Theodore H. Erickson, *Cluster Development* (Mimeographed paper, Board of Homeland Missions, UCC, April, 1969).

10. Report of the New Scotland Pilot Cluster, Synod of Albany, Reformed Church in America, 1974.

11. *Ibid.* Quotations throughout are taken from the summary, pp. 5-10.

12. Hassinger *et al.*, *A Comparison of Rural Churches*, pp. 23-24.

13. Hassinger, Benson, Dorsett and Holik, *The Church in Rural Missouri, 1967,* Research Bulletin 984, December, 1971, University of Missouri-Columbia, College of Agriculture, Agricultural Experiment Station, Columbia, Missouri, p. 27.

14. Final report by David J. Brown, Robert Haskins, and William Swisher, *Small Church Project* (New York: United Church Board for Homeland Ministries, June, 1977), p. 35.

Index

Administration
  in church clusters, 170-74
  of church program, 65-74
  in church types, 151-56
  compared to larger churches,
    24-26, 34-35
  frustrated by leadership, 56-57
  through goals and purposes,
    124-37
  maintaining independence of,
    174-75
  of social service, 99-100
  in tentmaking ministry, 168-70

Adaptability. *See* Stability

Character development
  through annual events, 106
  through caring, conserving,
    coping, 26, 177
  through goals, 134-37
  through heredity and environ-
    ment, 139-43
  through primary group, 32-33
  through program, 68
  through remembered history,
    88-91
  through unique experiences, 44

Church education
  for church leadership, 163-64
  through personal crises, 109-10
  in rhythm of seasons, 87
  through significant events, 108
  through Sunday school, 115-16
  teachers and materials, 65-66

Church neighborhoods
  declining, 39-40, 144
  growing, 80, 127, 141
  moving population, 52, 81, 94,
    177-78
  transitional, 141, 144

Church types
  cluster, 170-74
  ethnic, 112, 145-46
  high commitment,146-47
  local, 143-44
  moving, 81
  Old First, 39-40, 141, 145
  regional, 143-44
  rural, 112, 141
  stable, 144, 147-49
  suburban, 22-23, 48, 141
  town, 141
  urban, 141, 173

Clergy career
  denominational relationships,
    162-64
  in goal conflicts, 132-34
  pastor/people tensions, 62-74
  specialists, 23-24
  young sprinter, 86

Clergy spouse
  employment satisfaction, 64-65
  reaction to "stories," 72
  support of, 162

Conflict
  by breaking in, 54
  in church images, 88-89
  in church types, 151-54
  with goals, 127-30
  from intimacy, 41-42
  as natural socialization, 131-34
  pastor/people tensions, 62-74
  in primary group, 33

Denominations
  clergy advancement in, 63
  goal setting of, 126
  inheritance of, 140
  membership distribution of,
    21-25

Denominations *(continued)*
  needing one another, 156
  placement materials, 73
  viability of, 158-78
  view of small church in, 14-15,
    17, 48-49

Evaluation
  of achievements, 131
  of Christian love, 177
  of goals and purposes, 124-26
  of pastoral relationships and
    skills, 72-74
  of small church, 175-78
  of standards of success, 66-68
  of viable church, 164-67

Evangelism
  by adoption, 47-59
  in church types, 151-56
  through cluster churches, 173
  goals for newcomers, 125-26
  through personal crisis, 110
  through sharing a place, 96
  through small groups, 34

Family, sense of
  in church type, 146
  in crisis, 29
  in decisions, 128
  extended by adoption, 55-56
  feuds, 132-34
  in leadership, 130
  in overlapping groups, 154
  pastor as lover, 71-74
  in primary group, 32-33
  in shield, 89

Fund Raising
  through church types, 145-51
  for resident, ordained clergy,
    163
  turf stewardship, 116-19

Healthy church
  concern for, 40-41
  defined, 119-20
  healing ministries, 97
  importance of place, 95-96
  sometimes sick, 62

Identity
  through action, 34-35
  through events, 78-91, 105-20
  through history, 16-17, 23-24,
    32-33, 42-46, 56-59, 133-37,
    139-43, 163
  through objects, 43, 59, 92,
    100-102, 174
  through place, 32, 35-43, 93-
    103, 139-56

Leadership
  in church types, 145-51
  within the denomination, 174-
    75
  by denominational executives,
    158-61
  by gatekeepes, 56
  levels of, 130-31
  by lover, 71-74
  by matriarch, patriarch, 56-57
  pastor/people tensions, 62-74
  of storytellers, 86
  by tentmakers, 168-70
  by treasurer, 65

Location of church
  cluster office, 172
  effecting growth, 23-24
  turf types of churches, 139-56

Memory
  abuses of, 83-84
  biblical, 82-83
  in caring cell, 40-45
  in ethnic church, 146
  in goal setting, 134-35
  to make a memorial, 102-3
  to mark time, 106-9
  in people-places, 79-80
  in primary group, 32-33
  uses of, 85-86

Mission
  in church types,147, 149-50
  from heritage, 86
  statements of, 14-15
  See also Character development

Pastoral care and counseling
  as a caring church, 40-45

Pastoral care *(continued)*
in celebration, 136
in conflict with program, 69
in congregational identity, 115
in ethnic church, 146
in goal setting, 129-30
for lost membrs, 79
as lover, 71-74
a measure of membership, 48
in pastor's study, 61
in small church research, 53-54

Personal place
for healing, 95-96
implications for program, 40-45
for learning, 87
limits of caring, 47-51
in the meaning of land, 94-95
for naming of people, 78
pastor's study, 68-70
people-in-place, 35-39

Planning
budget, 117
in church type, 145-46
through goal setting, 126-28, 134-37
storytellers more important than planners, 86

Power
to accept members, 55-59
over goals and purposes, 130-37
in informal groups, 154-55
of objects and places, 101-2
in small church, 70-71
of spouse and treasurer, 64-65

Preaching
irony of good sermon, 64
source of satisfaction, 69

Primary group
defined, 32-35
conflict with secondary organization, 158-59

Small church
defined, 19, 35
perspectives on, 19-27

distinguished from larger churches: by the absence of new members, 47-51; by caring and surviving, 39-40; relationships, 21-25; by financial resources, 19; in growth by adoption, 56-57; in leadership style, 71-74; in pastoral relationships, 62; in program emphasis, 124-25; in similarities to other small churches, 139-40, 176; by single cell, 34-37
effective small church, defined, 17, 120, 121-22

Social action
attitudes of, 99-100
financed by expanding ministries, 113-14
of healing ministries, 97-99
from heritage, 86
through sharing a place, 96

Stability
through annual events, 110
autonomy, 174
through conflict, 132
in continuity, 125
through coping, 121
through effective programs, 65-68
in history of church, 16-17, 23-26
like human body, 115
through important places, 93-94
less open, more durable, 40
through membership continuity, 70
in primary group, 33
tenacious, stubborn, 21

Stewardship
through annual events, 105
in church types, 145-56
in conflict with denomination, 158-61, 164, 167-68
by conserving, 75-76
in finances, 15, 19, 20-21, 50 (*see also* Fund raising)
through goals, 130-31, 134-37

Stewardship *(continued)*
  in homecoming, 111-12
  of human energy, 67-68
  for independence, 174
  in pastoral relationship, 63-65
  through program, 155-56

Worship
  choreography of, 31

  communion in, 102-3
  gatekeepers' role at, 46
  listening to the pew, 44-45
  to mark time, 106-9
  for personal transitions, 109-10
  place as order, 35-39
  rhythm of, 84
  through things, 100-102
  as time remembered, 80